cooking
spanish

S0-AHC-083

cooking
spanish

John Newton

THUNDER BAY
P·R·E·S·S

San Diego, California

contents

simple and satisfying

The last ten years or so have seen a culinary revolution taking place in Spain. But as much as we may admire Spain's new wave of cooking, *la nueva cocina*, deep in the heart and not so deep in the palate lies a yearning for the earthy, gutsy, and blatantly honest home cooking that you find across the country. These traditional cuisines are the results of geography, history, and personality. You will note that the plural is used—cuisines—and that is because Spanish food differs markedly from end to end and side to side of the Iberian Peninsula. As it should: that peninsula stretches north to south, from France to Africa, and east to west, from the Mediterranean to the Atlantic. A brief circumnavigation of the peninsula reveals something of the history of its ingredients and dishes.

The cooking of the northeastern corner of Spain, the Basque countries, is heavily influenced by its geography. In the Basque capital, San Sebastían, you will find some of the best seafood in Spain—from both the Mediterranean and the Atlantic—as well as the famed vegetables of Navarra, and, from across the French border, foie gras from the Landes and truffles from the Périgord. One ingredient can be directly sourced to the Basques, and that is *bacalao*, salted and dried cod. Intrepid Basque whalers first brought *bacalao* back from the Canadian Newfoundland coast a thousand years ago.

Moving south and east into Catalonia, the influence of the French neighbors can be detected—for instance, in dishes where chicken liver pâté, *mousse de fetge*, is used—but so too can that of the Moors. Catalans share, with other northerners, a love for cooler-climate rustic dishes using beans and sausage, such as chickpeas with chorizo, mostly deriving from pre-Moorish times and springing from villages of farmer peasants. Of definite Moorish origin is the introduction of rice, the basis for hundreds of dishes, only one of which is paella. This famous dish originated in the Catalan speaking province of Valencia and consisted of rice, vegetables, and chicken, frogs, or snails. These days, paella often also features fish and seafood caught off the Catalan coast.

Travel inland to the capital, Madrid, and you encounter the harsh and beautiful landscape of the South and North Mesetas (plateaus). Here, you enter the realm of roast suckling pig and lamb, and the *cocido Madrileño*, a slow-cooked stew of chickpeas and meat. The North Meseta is covered in wheat fields, forests of pine, beech, and oak, and grazing flocks of merino sheep. The harsher South Meseta is the landscape of Don Quixote and the home of the wild boar and the Manchego sheep, as well as vineyards and wheat fields.

RECORTES

Back on the eastern coast, from Murcia to Andalusia, the major influences are the Moorish past and the sea. In the case of Andalusia, the sea refers to both the Mediterranean and the Atlantic. Here, numerous seafood dishes, like *sardinas Murciana* and *calamares a la plancha*, reveal the importance of the bounty from the Mediterranean. Spain's famous cold soups—gazpacho, *salmorejo*, *porra*, and *ajo blanco*—also derive from these hot southern regions.

It is here in Andalusia that the rich heritage of the Moorish occupation is most in evidence. The Arabs brought with them not just food but a culture. Their reign, from 711 to 1492, coincided with the highest point of Islamic civilization, and their impact on Spanish architecture, agriculture, music, landscape gardening, and gastronomy is still evident some five hundred years after their departure. It is hard to imagine a Spain without oranges, roses, and saffron, all gifts of the Moors.

Inland and to the north, we come to the Andalusian region of Huelva, home of the famous lamb stew, *caldereta del condado*, and the even more famous *pata negra*, the black Iberian pig. The pig in all its forms is the basis of the cuisine of Extremadura, Spain's westernmost and most isolated province, whose border with Portugal is also a culinary influence.

The seafood province of Spain is Galicia, nestled in the country's cool and rainy northwestern corner. From here come dishes such as *pulpo gallego* (boiled octopus) and delicacies like *percebes* (goose barnacles). Heading east along the Cantabrian coast, we come to the mountainous province of Asturias, home to the most famous sausage and bean dish of all, *fabada Asturiana*. Among the mountains known as the Picos de Europa, some of the world's finest blue cheeses are made, including Cabrales and Picon. Last, but certainly not least, on our culinary journey is the rugged and fertile northeastern province of Navarra. The rivers of this mountainous province teem with trout and salmon. The region is also famed throughout Spain for its vegetables, particularly asparagus and the local red bell pepper—*el pimiento del piquillo*.

On this voyage around the peninsula, we have forgotten one vital contribution to the cuisines of Spain: the Spanish character. Divided by distance, language, and background, the Spanish are united by their love of good food, good wine, and conversation. Out of these qualities springs the tapas tradition. The recipes in this book have been organized into sections based either on the Spanish way of life—tapas traditions and pastries and sweets—or on the country's geography: the coastline and plains and mountains. Along the way, you will become acquainted with the techniques, ingredients, and influences that make Spanish dishes some of the most fascinating and varied in Europe.

tapas traditions

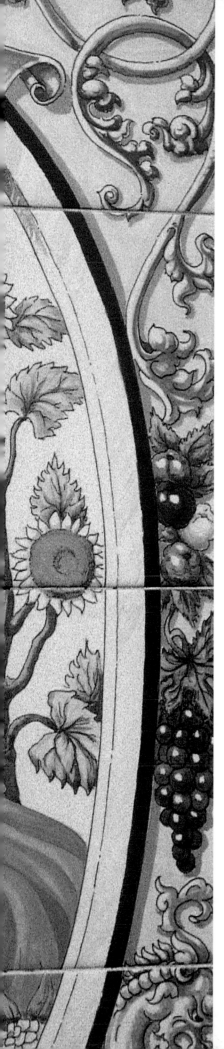

In even the most ordinary tapas bar (or *tasca*) in a small town or one of the outer barrios (suburbs) of a large town, you are able to choose from a dazzling array of tapas. Laid out along the bar behind a glass case will be piles of black mussels, curls of garlicky shrimp, and shimmering stacks of sardines. Hanging overhead are succulent legs of *jamón serrano* (cured ham), strings of sausages, chilies like firecrackers, and plump, dried red bell peppers.

Without a word of Spanish, you can order by pointing at such dishes as *gambas al ajillo*, sizzling clay pots of shrimp cooked in olive oil and immoral quantities of garlic, and *chorizo en sidra*, a specialty from the mountainous northern province of Asturias. If you have any room, a slice of tortilla is as Spanish, as earthy, and as rich as flamenco.

However, there is much more to tapas than an array of alluring dishes. Generally eaten standing up, tapas is a way of life as much as a way of eating, a convivial way to fill the gap between the end of work and the beginning of the evening meal; a leisurely stroll with friends, from bar to bar, sipping tiny glasses of chilled *fino* (sherry) or beer between delicious mouthfuls. Tapas is the fast food of the gods.

In the beginning, tapas were free snacks handed out by the innkeepers of Andalusia, in the country's south, with the evening glass of chilled sherry or wine. Nothing elaborate, just a slice of chorizo sausage or Manchego cheese on a hunk of coarse bread. Stop for a glass of wine or a beer in a bodega (inn) or bar in Andalusia today, and chances are you will be given such a snack.

The noun "tapas" is from the verb *tapear* (to cover), alluding to the old Andalusian habit of covering one's glass with a slice of sausage or ham. Today, the habit of wandering from bar to bar is known in the south of Spain as *tapeando*, literally, "tapasing." In the northern Basque country, tapas are called *pinchos* (skewers), as many northern Spanish tapas are skewered, and the tapas crawl is known as the *chiquiteo* or, in the Basque language, *txikiteo*.

But wherever you find it, the tapas bar will be packed with locals arguing about politics and soccer as they eat and drink. Go in for a drink or a coffee, or both, and then stay for as long as you like, watching the passersby, brushing up on your Spanish, listening to the old men in the corner passing conversation around the table carefully, as though it were a precious vessel—and in Spain, it is: Miguel de Unamuno, philosopher, poet, novelist, and critic, wrote that "Spanish culture is to be found in the cafés more often than the universities."

chili olives..fills a 4-cup jar

IN EVERY BAR IN SPAIN YOU WILL FIND BOWLS OF OLIVES, GREEN OR BLACK, THE BEST CURED IN BRINE FOR UP TO SIX MONTHS. THIS DELIGHTFUL DISH HAS OLIVES FROM THE OLD WORLD, CHILIES FROM THE NEW, AND SPICES FROM THE EAST—A MIX OF TEXTURES AND FLAVORS THAT WILL PLEASE THE MOST JADED OF TASTE BUDS.

garlic	3 cloves, thinly sliced
vinegar or lemon juice	3 tablespoons
cured (wrinkled) black olives	3 cups
Italian parsley	¼ cup chopped
chili flakes	4 teaspoons
coriander seeds	1 tablespoon, crushed
cumin seeds	2 teaspoons, crushed
olive oil	2 cups

Soak the garlic slices in the vinegar or lemon juice for 24 hours. Drain and mix the garlic in a small bowl with the olives, parsley, chili flakes, coriander, and cumin.

Sterilize a 4-cup, wide-necked jar by rinsing it well in boiling water, then leaving it to dry in a warm oven (don't dry it with a dish towel).

Spoon the olives into the jar and pour in the olive oil. Seal and marinate in the refrigerator for up to two weeks before serving at room temperature. The olives will keep for one month if stored in the refrigerator.

Spanish life and cuisine are lubricated by the juice from the fruit of the olive tree. Having arrived in Spain around 1000 BC with the Phoenicians, the olive tree was further cultivated by the Romans, but its place at the heart of Spanish cooking was really consolidated by the Moors. Today, the farther south you travel, the more the landscape is carpeted with row upon row of olive trees. This is because the Moors never really made inroads into the cooler northern parts of Spain. They found the climate inhospitable and stayed mainly in the south, as did the olive tree. Consequently, the traditional dishes of the north feature lard and butter, and those of the south, olive oil.

alcachofas en vinagreta aromática

THIS TAPAS, BASED ON THE GLOBE ARTICHOKE IN A DELICIOUS SWEET-SOUR SAUCE, COMES WITH ITS OWN HANDLE, THE STALK—PERFECT FOR EASY EATING AT THE TAPAS BAR. ARTICHOKES WERE FIRST INTRODUCED INTO SPAIN BY THE ARABS IN THE MID-FIFTEENTH CENTURY, AND THEIR USE OFTEN REFLECTS THIS HERITAGE.

lemon juice	3 tablespoons
globe artichokes	4 large
garlic	2 cloves, crushed
oregano	1 teaspoon finely chopped
ground cumin	½ teaspoon
ground coriander	½ teaspoon
chili flakes	a pinch
sherry vinegar	1 tablespoon
olive oil	¼ cup

Add the lemon juice to a large bowl of cold water. Trim the artichokes, cutting off the stalks to within 2 inches of the base of each artichoke and removing the tough outer leaves. Cut off the top quarter of the leaves from each artichoke. Slice each artichoke in half from top to base, or into quarters if very large. Remove each small, furry choke with a teaspoon, then place each artichoke piece in the bowl of acidulated water to prevent it from discoloring while you prepare the rest.

Bring a large, nonaluminum saucepan of water to a boil, add the artichokes and a teaspoon of salt, and simmer for 20 minutes or until tender. (The cooking time will depend on the size of the artichoke.) Test by pressing a skewer into the base. If cooked, the artichokes will be soft and give little resistance. Strain, then drain the artichoke pieces on their cut side while cooling.

Combine the garlic, oregano, cumin, coriander, and chili flakes in a bowl. Season with a little salt and pepper and blend in the vinegar. Beating constantly, slowly and steadily add the olive oil to form an emulsion. This step can be done in a food processor.

Arrange the artichokes in a row on a platter. Pour the dressing over the top and allow to cool completely before serving.

Prepare the artichokes by removing the tough outer leaves.

Use a teaspoon to remove the furry choke from each artichoke.

jerez

We should make one thing perfectly clear right from the start. Sherry, the anglicization of **Jerez** (pronounced "he-reth") is produced only in Spain, and only in what is known as the "Sherry Triangle"—a very small segment of southern Andalusia bounded by the towns of Jerez de la Frontera, Puerto de Santa María, and Sanlúcar de Barrameda, the last two situated on Spain's Atlantic coast. Anything called "sherry" that is not produced in this region is not sherry at all, and may be a more or less pleasant imitation.

The production of sherry is a complex process. What starts out as a fairly ordinary dry white wine is aged using the *solera* system. Basically, a series of wines in casks, graded by age, are blended from small amounts of the oldest to larger amounts of the youngest.

If the sherry is to be a fino, its production also includes time spent under *flor* (flower), a growth of yeasts on the wine's surface. Finally, all sherry is fortified with brandy.

The variety and complexity of flavors of the various styles of sherry—from the steely dry fino, which should always be served chilled, or an aged and nutty *oloroso* to the lip-smacking richness of the single grape variety, Pedro Ximénez—are a revelation to those used to only the warm, sickly cream sherry served by maiden aunts.

When to drink sherry? Well, in Andalusia, fino is treated as a white wine and is drunk throughout the meal—with trout or chicken, for example. Fino with oysters is another match made in heaven. But more often, it is drunk as an apéritif, simply with olives and cheese or with tapas. The same goes for the other dry sherry, manzanilla. Like fino, it should always be served chilled and fresh. These styles do not age well.

A dry amontillado or palo cortado is often served with soup, but the bigger, sweeter, and heavier styles are best left to the end of the meal—serve the oldest and "brownest" of olorosos or amontillados with dessert or cheese, and Pedro Ximénez with the richest of sweet dishes.

If you become a true aficionado, you will want to experiment with different sherries with every course, as is done in many modern restaurants in Andalusia.

Sherry is also used extensively in cooking, most notably in *riñones en Jerez* (kidneys in sherry sauce). In Andalusia, a splash of fino is often added to gazpacho.

chickpeas with chorizo .... serves 6

THIS COMBINATION OF TWO EMBLEMATIC INGREDIENTS OF SPANISH COOKING PROVIDES A SIMPLE BUT SATISFYING AND HEARTY TAPAS DISH. CHORIZO, AN OFTEN FIERY SAUSAGE OF PORK AND *PIMENTÓN*, IS EATEN ACROSS SPAIN, FROM SAN SEBASTÍAN TO SEVILLE, BARCELONA TO BADAJOZ.

dried chickpeas	3/4 cup
bay leaf	1
cloves	4
cinnamon stick	1
chicken stock	3 cups
olive oil	3 tablespoons
onion	1, finely chopped
garlic	1 clove, crushed
dried thyme	a pinch
chorizo	13 oz., chopped into cubes slightly larger than the chickpeas
Italian parsley	4 teaspoons chopped

Put the chickpeas in a large bowl, cover with water, and soak overnight. Drain, then put in a large saucepan with the bay leaf, cloves, cinnamon stick, and stock. Cover completely with water, bring to a boil, and then reduce the heat and simmer for 1 hour, or until the chickpeas are tender. If they need more time, add a little more water. There should be just a little liquid left in the pan. Drain and remove the bay leaf, cloves, and cinnamon stick.

Heat the oil in a large frying pan, add the onion, and cook over medium heat for 3 minutes or until translucent. Add the garlic and thyme and cook, stirring, for 1 minute. Increase the heat to medium-high, add the chorizo, and cook for 3 minutes.

Add the chickpeas to the frying pan, mix well, and then stir over medium heat until they are heated through. Remove from the heat and mix through the parsley. Taste before seasoning with salt and freshly ground black pepper. This dish is equally delicious served hot or at room temperature.

The chickpea, or garbanzo bean, is another legacy of the Moorish occupation of Spain. Though wholeheartedly adopted in that country, it was so foreign to the rest of Europe that one nineteenth-century writer could only describe it as "a pea with an only too successful ambition to be a bean." Chickpeas are not, as in the Middle East, crushed (to make hummus) or, as in India, ground (to make chickpea flour), but soaked, stewed, and eaten whole. They are the most important legume in Spain and feature in such quintessentially Spanish dishes as *olla gitana* (gypsy stew) and *cocido Madrileño*.

albóndigas . . . . serves 6

ALL OVER THE WORLD YOU WILL FIND MEATBALLS, BUT NONE AS FLAVORFUL AS THE *ALBÓNDIGA* OF SPAIN. ORIGINALLY MOORISH—ALL SPANISH WORDS STARTING WITH "AL" ARE ARABIC IN ORIGIN—THESE MEATBALLS ARE RECOGNIZABLE THROUGH THEIR RICH SAUCE, GOLDEN-FRIED APPEARANCE, AND GENEROUS USE OF SPICES.

ground pork	6 oz.
ground veal	6 oz.
garlic	3 cloves, crushed
dry breadcrumbs	1/3 cup
ground coriander	1 teaspoon
ground nutmeg	1 teaspoon
ground cumin	1 teaspoon
ground cinnamon	a pinch
egg	1
olive oil	3 tablespoons

spicy tomato sauce

olive oil	4 teaspoons
onion	1, chopped
garlic	1 clove, crushed
dry white wine	1/2 cup
good-quality crushed tomatoes	14-oz. can
tomato paste	4 teaspoons
chicken stock	1/2 cup
cayenne pepper	1/2 teaspoon
fresh or frozen peas	1/2 cup

Combine the pork, veal, garlic, breadcrumbs, spices, egg, and some salt and pepper in a bowl. Mix by hand until the mixture is smooth and leaves the side of the bowl. Refrigerate, covered, for 30 minutes.

Roll tablespoons of the mixture into balls. Heat 4 teaspoons olive oil in a frying pan and toss half the meatballs over medium-high heat for 2–3 minutes or until browned. Drain on paper towels. Add the remaining oil, if necessary, and brown the rest of the meatballs. Drain on paper towels.

To make the spicy tomato sauce, heat the oil in a frying pan over medium heat and add the onion. Cook, stirring occasionally, for 3 minutes or until soft and translucent. Add the garlic and cook for 1 minute. Increase the heat to high, add the wine, and boil for 1 minute. Add the crushed tomatoes, tomato paste, and stock and simmer for 10 minutes. Stir in the cayenne pepper, peas, and meatballs and gently simmer for 5–10 minutes or until the sauce is thick. Serve hot.

Put the meatball ingredients in a large bowl and stir to combine.

Form the mixture into balls, then cook until brown all over.

Add the cayenne pepper to the spicy tomato sauce and simmer.

three ways with garlic

YOUR FIRST SMELL OF SPAIN IS GARLIC. YOUR FIRST TASTE OF SPANISH FOOD IS PROBABLY *GAMBAS AL AJILLO* (GARLIC SHRIMP). GARLIC IN SPAIN IS NOT USED AS A DELICATE ADDITION WITH WHICH TO FLAVOR FOOD, BUT AS A VEGETABLE IN ITS OWN RIGHT. CUT GARLIC IS RUBBED ONTO BREAD, WHOLE CLOVES ARE THROWN INTO STEWS, GARLIC CHIPS ARE STREWN OVER FRIED FISH, AND DISHES SUCH AS *SOPA DE AJOS* AND *AJO BLANCO* ARE CHILLED SOUPS WHOSE MAIN INGREDIENT IS, OF COURSE, GARLIC.

gambas al ajillo

Preheat the oven to 500°F. Peel 2 lb. 12 oz. uncooked shrimp, leaving the tails intact. Pull out the vein from the back, starting at the head. Cut a slit down the back of each shrimp. Divide 1 cup olive oil among four 2-cup cast-iron pots. Crush 8 garlic cloves and divide half among the pots. Put the pots on a baking sheet and heat in the oven for 10 minutes or until the mixture is bubbling. Remove from the oven and divide the shrimp and remaining garlic among the pots. Return to the oven for 5 minutes or until the shrimp are cooked. Stir in 2 thinly sliced scallions. Season to taste. Serve with crusty bread to mop up the juices. Serves 4.

pan con tomate

Slice 1 crusty bread stick diagonally, and halve 6 garlic cloves and 3 vine-ripened tomatoes. Toast the slices very lightly. Rub them on one side with a cut garlic clove, then rub with half a tomato, squeezing the juice onto the bread. Season with a little salt and drizzle with extra-virgin olive oil. Serve as part of a tapas or as a simple snack. Serves 6.

champiñones al ajillo

Crush 4 garlic cloves and finely slice 2 more. Finely chop a quarter of a long red chili. Finely slice 10 cups button, Swiss brown, or pine mushrooms. Sprinkle 2 tablespoons lemon juice over the mushrooms. Heat 1/4 cup olive oil in a large frying pan and add the crushed garlic and chopped chili. Stir over medium-high heat for 10 seconds, then add the mushrooms. Season and cook, stirring often, for 8–10 minutes. Stir in the sliced garlic and 2 teaspoons chopped Italian parsley and cook for another minute. Serve hot. Serves 4.

patatas bravas .... serves 6

THIS IS A DISH RARELY SEEN OUTSIDE THE TAPAS BAR, THAT CAN, LIKE THE SIMPLE TORTILLA, REVEAL THE QUALITY OF THE REST OF THE TAPAS AT THE BAR. THE TELLTALE SIGNS OF A GOOD PATATAS BRAVAS ARE POTATOES THAT ARE FIRM TO THE MOUTH BUT NOT STARCHY, AND A SAUCE THAT IS DEEPLY SPICY.

waxy potatoes, such as desiree	6 medium
oil	for deep-frying
plum tomatoes	4 medium
olive oil	3 tablespoons
red onion	1/4, finely chopped
garlic	2 cloves, crushed
sweet *pimentón* (paprika)	1 tablespoon
cayenne pepper	1/4 teaspoon
bay leaf	1
sugar	1 teaspoon
Italian parsley	4 teaspoons chopped, to garnish, optional

Peel the potatoes, then cut them into 3/4-inch cubes. Rinse, then drain well and pat dry. Fill a deep-fat fryer or large, heavy-based saucepan one-third full of oil and heat to 350°F or until a cube of bread dropped into the oil browns in 15 seconds. Cook the potatoes in batches for 5 minutes or until golden. Drain well on paper towels. Do not discard the oil.

Score a cross in the base of each tomato. Put in a saucepan of boiling water for 10 seconds, then plunge into cold water and peel the skin away from the cross. Chop the flesh.

Heat the olive oil in a saucepan over medium heat and cook the onion for 3 minutes or until softened. Add the garlic, *pimentón*, and cayenne pepper, and cook for 1–2 minutes or until fragrant.

Add the chopped tomatoes, bay leaf, sugar, and 1/3 cup water and cook, stirring occasionally, for 20 minutes or until thick and pulpy. Cool slightly and remove the bay leaf. Blend in a food processor until smooth, adding a little water if necessary. Before serving, return the sauce to the saucepan and simmer over low heat for 2 minutes or until heated through. Season well.

Reheat the oil to 350°F and cook the potatoes again, in batches, for 2 minutes or until very crisp and golden. Drain on paper towels. This second frying makes the potatoes extra crispy and keeps the sauce from soaking in immediately. Put on a platter and cover with the sauce. Garnish with the parsley, if using, and serve.

Cut a cross in the tomatoes, then blanch and peel the skin away.

Cook the potatoes a second time in the oil until crisp and golden.

croquetas

THESE LITTLE DEEP-FRIED SNACKS ARE LOVED FOR THEIR SUBLIME SYMPHONY OF CRUNCHY OUTSIDE AND CREAMY INSIDE, WHICH, IF PERFECT, WILL EXPLODE IN THE MOUTH WITH RICH FLAVOR—IN THIS CASE, OF *JAMÓN*.

butter	6 tablespoons
onion	1 small, finely chopped
open cap mushrooms	2 medium, finely chopped
all-purpose flour	1½ cups
milk	1 cup
chicken stock	¾ cup
jamón or prosciutto	4 oz., finely chopped
eggs	2, lightly beaten
dry breadcrumbs	½ cup
oil	for deep-frying

Melt the butter in a saucepan over low heat, add the onion, and cook for 5 minutes or until translucent. Add the mushrooms and cook over low heat, stirring occasionally, for 5 minutes. Add 1 cup of the flour and stir over medium-low heat for 1 minute, or until the mixture is dry and crumbly and begins to change color. Remove from the heat and gradually add the milk, stirring until smooth. Stir in the stock and return to the heat, stirring until the mixture boils and thickens. Stir in the ham and some freshly ground black pepper, then transfer the mixture to a bowl to cool for 2 hours.

Roll heaping tablespoons of the mixture into croquette shapes about 2½ inches long. Put the remaining flour, beaten egg, and breadcrumbs into three shallow bowls. Toss the croquettes in the flour, dip in the egg, allowing the excess to drain away, then roll in the breadcrumbs. Put on a baking sheet and refrigerate for about 30 minutes.

Fill a deep, heavy-based saucepan one-third full of oil and heat to 325°F or until a cube of bread dropped into the oil browns in 20 seconds. Add the croquettes in batches and deep-fry for 3 minutes, turning, until brown. Drain well. Serve hot.

To make the *croquetas*, combine the flour with the mushrooms.

Roll the mixture into croquette shapes in your hands.

Chill the breadcrumb-coated *croquetas* before cooking.

three ways with bell peppers

THE SPANISH NAME FOR BELL PEPPER IS *PIMIENTO*. IT COMMEMORATES COLUMBUS'S MISTAKEN BELIEF THAT HE WAS FORGING A NEW ROUTE TO THE EAST, THE HOME OF SPICES SUCH AS BLACK PEPPER, WHICH THE SPANIARDS CALLED *PIMIENTA*. THE NEW ENDING, THE MASCULINE "O," POINTED TO THE MORE POWERFUL HEAT OF THE CHILI PEPPER HE FOUND IN THE AMERICAS. TO CONFUSE MATTERS EVEN MORE, "PIMIENTO" NOW MEANS ALL FORMS OF BELL PEPPER, INCLUDING THE CHILI, WHICH IS KNOWN AS *EL PIMIENTO PICANTE*—HOT PEPPER.

marinated bell peppers

Preheat the broiler. Cut 3 red bell peppers into quarters, remove the seeds and membrane, and broil, skin side up, until the skin blackens and blisters. Cool in a plastic bag, then peel. Slice thinly, then put in a bowl with 3 thyme sprigs, 1 thinly sliced garlic clove, 2 teaspoons roughly chopped Italian parsley, 1 bay leaf, and 1 sliced scallion. Mix well. Whisk together 1 teaspoon sweet *pimentón* (paprika), 1/4 cup extra-virgin olive oil, 3 tablespoons red wine vinegar, and some salt and freshly ground black pepper. Pour over the bell pepper mixture and toss to combine. Cover and refrigerate for at least 3 hours or preferably overnight. Remove from the refrigerator about 30 minutes before serving. Serves 6.

spanish vegetable stew

Heat 1/2 cup extra-virgin olive oil in a flameproof casserole dish. Add 1 chopped large onion and cook over medium heat for 5 minutes, then add 3 finely chopped garlic cloves. Add 2 seeded and roughly diced green bell peppers and 2 peeled and roughly diced zucchini and cook over low heat for 5 minutes. Add 2 lb. 4 oz. peeled and coarsely diced vine-ripened tomatoes. Season with salt and simmer over low heat for 30 minutes or until the flavors blend, stirring to prevent the vegetables from sticking to the bottom of the dish. Serve with canned tuna or scrambled or hard-boiled eggs, or as a tapas, on top of a slice of toasted crusty bread with an anchovy to garnish. Serves 6.

red bell pepper salad

Preheat the oven to 400°F. Put 4 medium red bell peppers in a roasting pan and rub all over with olive oil. Add 3 large unpeeled garlic cloves and 1 large beefsteak tomato and cook for 15 minutes. Remove the garlic and the tomato, turn the bell peppers, and cook for an additional 15 minutes. Skin, seed, and chop the tomato flesh, reserving the juice. Peel the garlic. Put the bell peppers in a bag to cool, then peel, seed, and slice the flesh into strips, reserving the juice. Arrange the bell pepper strips on a serving dish. Pound or process the garlic and tomatoes to a paste. Add 1/3 cup extra-virgin olive oil, 1 teaspoon sherry vinegar, and the reserved tomato and bell pepper juices and mix through. Pour the dressing over the bell pepper and sprinkle with 4 teaspoons chopped Italian parsley. Serves 4.

tuna empanadas . . . . makes 24

ORIGINALLY FROM GALICIA, THE EMPANADA IS SPAIN'S VERSION OF THE PIE. IT WOULD HAVE BEEN A PRACTICAL
AND SATISFYING SNACK FOR THE HARDY GALICIANS, WHO FOR CENTURIES HAVE BEEN FARMERS AND FISHERMEN
IN A DIFFICULT LANDSCAPE. TODAY, IT COMES WITH A VARIETY OF FILLINGS, BUT THE TUNA VERSION IS A FAVORITE.

all-purpose flour	3¼ cups, plus extra, for rolling
butter	5½ tablespoons, softened
eggs	3, one lightly beaten
white wine	¼ cup

filling

olive oil	4 teaspoons
onion	1 small, finely diced
tomato paste	2 teaspoons
canned tomatoes	½ cup, chopped
tuna	3-oz. can, drained
roasted bell pepper	2 tablespoons chopped
Italian parsley	3 tablespoons chopped

Sift the flour and 1 teaspoon salt into a large bowl. Rub the butter into the flour until the mixture resembles fine breadcrumbs. Combine the 2 whole eggs and the wine and add to the bowl, cutting the liquid in with a flat-bladed knife to form a dough. Turn onto a lightly floured surface and gather together into a smooth ball (do not knead or you will end up with tough pastry). Cover with plastic wrap and refrigerate for 30 minutes.

To make the filling, heat the olive oil in a frying pan over medium heat and cook the onion for about 5 minutes or until translucent. Add the tomato paste and chopped tomatoes and cook for about 10 minutes or until thick. Add the tuna, roasted bell pepper, and parsley and season well.

Preheat the oven to 375°F. Dust a work surface with a little extra flour. Roll out half the pastry to a thickness of 1/16 inch. Using a 4-inch cutter, cut into 12 rounds. Put a heaping tablespoon of filling on each round, fold over, brush the edges with water, and then gently pinch to seal. Continue with the remaining rounds, then repeat with the remaining dough and filling to make 24 empanadas.

Transfer to a lightly oiled baking sheet and brush each empanada with the beaten egg. Bake for about 30 minutes or until golden. Serve warm or cold.

Use a flat-bladed knife to cut the egg mixture into the flour.

Fold each pastry round in half, encasing the filling.

Pinch the pastry edges together with your fingers, to seal.

stuffed mussels .... makes 18

CHEAPER AND MORE VERSATILE THAN THEIR MOLLUSK RELATION, THE OYSTER, MUSSELS LEND THEMSELVES TO A GREAT NUMBER OF PREPARATIONS, INCLUDING THIS DELICIOUSLY CRUNCHY, GARLICKY DISH.

black mussels	18
olive oil	2 teaspoons
scallions	2, finely chopped
garlic	1 clove, crushed
tomato paste	4 teaspoons
lemon juice	2 teaspoons
Italian parsley	1/3 cup chopped
dry breadcrumbs	3/4 cup
eggs	2, beaten
oil	for deep-frying

white sauce

butter	1 1/2 tablespoons
all-purpose flour	2 tablespoons
milk	3 tablespoons

Scrub the mussels and remove the hairy beards. Discard any open mussels that don't close when tapped on the counter. Bring 1 cup water to a boil in a saucepan, add the mussels, and then cover and cook for 3–4 minutes, shaking the pan occasionally, until the mussels have just opened. Remove them from the pan as soon as they open. Strain the liquid into a jar until you have 1/3 cup and reserve. Discard any unopened mussels. Remove the mussels from their shells and discard one half shell from each. Finely chop the mussel meat.

Heat the olive oil in a frying pan, add the scallions, and cook for 1 minute. Add the garlic and cook for an additional minute. Stir in the mussels, tomato paste, lemon juice, half the parsley, and some salt and freshly ground black pepper. Set aside to cool.

To make the white sauce, melt the butter in a saucepan over low heat. Add the flour and cook for about 1 minute or until pale and foaming. Remove from the heat and gradually whisk in the reserved mussel liquid, the milk, and some freshly ground black pepper. Return to the heat and cook, stirring, for 1 minute, or until the sauce boils and thickens. Reduce the heat and simmer for 2 minutes. Allow to cool.

Spoon the mussel mixture into the shells. Top each with some of the white sauce, heaping the mixture neatly.

Combine the breadcrumbs and remaining parsley on a plate. Dip the mussels in the beaten egg, then press in the crumbs to cover the top. Fill a deep, heavy-based saucepan one-third full of oil and heat to 350°F or until a cube of bread browns in 15 seconds. Cook the mussels in batches for 10–15 seconds or until lightly browned. Remove with a slotted spoon and drain well. Serve hot.

Cook the mussels in boiling water, lifting them out as they open.

Smooth the white sauce over the mussel mixture in each shell.

three ways with meat tapas

CARNIVORES ARE WELL LOOKED AFTER IN SPAIN, WITH A WIDE CHOICE OF MEATS SERVED EVERYWHERE. GOAT IS POPULAR, AS ARE RABBIT AND HARE. IN THE TOWNS OF SEPÚLVEDA IN SEGOVIA AND ARANDA DE DUERO IN BURGOS, FOR EXAMPLE, WHOLE STREETS ARE LINED WITH RESTAURANTS DEVOTED TO ROASTED SUCKLING PIG AND LAMB. EVEN THE FIGHTING BULLS, ONCE VANQUISHED, END UP IN THE COOKING POT. IN SPITE OF THE SPANISH FONDNESS FOR VEGETABLES AND LEGUMES, THESE TOO ARE INVARIABLY SERVED WITH MEAT, SUCH AS BEANS WITH HAM.

chorizo in apple cider sauce

Heat ¼ cup olive oil in a saucepan over low heat. Add 1 finely chopped small onion and cook for 3 minutes or until soft, stirring occasionally. Add 1½ teaspoons sweet *pimentón* (paprika) and cook for 1 minute. Increase the heat to medium, add ½ cup dry hard apple cider, ¼ cup chicken stock, and 1 bay leaf to the pan, and bring to a boil. Reduce the heat and simmer for 5 minutes. Slice 10 oz. chorizo on the diagonal, add to the pan, and simmer for 5 minutes or until the sauce has reduced slightly. Stir in 2 teaspoons sherry vinegar and 2 teaspoons chopped Italian parsley. Serve hot. Serves 4.

fava beans with *jamón*

Melt 1½ tablespoons butter in a large saucepan and add 1 finely chopped onion, 6 oz. roughly chopped *jamón* or prosciutto, and 2 crushed garlic cloves. Cook over medium heat for 5 minutes, stirring often, until the onion softens. Add 3 cups fresh or frozen fava beans and ½ cup dry white wine and cook over high heat until reduced by half. Add ¾ cup chicken stock, reduce the heat, cover, and cook for about 10 minutes. Uncover and simmer for an additional 10 minutes. Serve warm as a tapas dish with crusty bread or hot as a side dish. Serves 4.

chicken in garlic sauce

Trim any excess fat from 2 lb. 4 oz. chicken thigh fillets and cut the thighs into thirds. Combine 4 teaspoons sweet *pimentón* (paprika) with some salt and freshly ground black pepper in a bowl, add the chicken, and toss to coat. Heat 4 teaspoons olive oil in a large frying pan over high heat and cook 8 unpeeled garlic cloves for 1–2 minutes or until brown. Remove from the pan. Cook the chicken in batches for 5 minutes or until brown all over. Return all the chicken to the pan, add ¼ cup dry sherry, boil for 30 seconds, and then add ½ cup chicken stock and 1 bay leaf. Reduce the heat to low and simmer, covered, for about 10 minutes. Meanwhile, squeeze the garlic pulp into a mortar or small bowl. Add 3 tablespoons chopped Italian parsley and pound with the pestle or mix with a fork to form a paste. Stir into the chicken, then cover and cook for 10 minutes or until tender. Serve hot. Serves 6.

buñuelos de bacalao

THESE EXQUISITE LITTLE FRITTERS ARE A CLASSIC CATALAN TAPAS DISH AND ARE A TESTAMENT TO THE ENDURING APPEAL OF *BACALAO*, FIRST BROUGHT TO SPAIN BY BASQUE FISHERMEN. SUCH IS THE POPULARITY OF THIS DISH THAT IT IS EVEN SERVED AS AN APPETIZER IN SOME OF THE BETTER RESTAURANTS.

bacalao (salt cod)	1 lb. 2 oz.
potato	1 large, unpeeled
milk	3 tablespoons
olive oil	1/4 cup
onion	1 small, finely chopped
garlic	2 cloves, crushed
self-rising flour	1/4 cup
eggs	2, separated
Italian parsley	4 teaspoons chopped
oil	for deep-frying

Soak the *bacalao* in plenty of cold water for about 20 hours, changing the water four or five times to remove excess saltiness. Cook the potato in a saucepan of boiling water for 20 minutes or until soft. When cool, peel and mash in a bowl with the milk and 3 tablespoons of the olive oil.

Drain the *bacalao*, cut into large pieces, and put in a saucepan. Cover with water, bring to a boil over high heat, reduce the heat to low—it should be no hotter than 150°F—and poach for 35–45 minutes or until the fish is soft and there is a froth on the surface. Drain. When cool enough to handle, remove the skin and any bones, then mash the flesh well with a fork until flaky.

Heat the remaining oil in a small frying pan and cook the onion over medium heat for 5 minutes or until softened and starting to brown. Add the garlic and cook for 1 minute. Remove the pan from the heat.

Combine the potato, *bacalao*, onion mixture, flour, egg yolks, and parsley in a bowl and season. Whisk the egg whites until stiff, then fold into the mixture. Fill a deep-fat fryer or heavy-based saucepan one-third full of olive oil and heat to 375°F or until a cube of bread dropped into the oil browns in 10 seconds. Drop heaping tablespoons of the mixture into the oil and cook, turning once, for 2–3 minutes or until puffed and golden. Drain well and serve immediately.

russian salad .... serves 4 to 6

THIS DELICIOUS DISH OFFERS UP ONE OF THE GREAT MYSTERIES OF LIFE. WHY IS A GARLICKY POTATO AND ARTICHOKE SALAD HAILING FROM RUSSIA TO BE FOUND IN EVERY TAPAS BAR IN SPAIN? NO MATTER, IT'S AN IDEAL ACCOMPANIMENT TO A REFRESHING GLASS OF COLD BEER.

canned artichoke hearts	3
waxy potatoes, such as desiree	3, unpeeled
baby green beans	1 1/2 cups, trimmed and cut into 1/2-inch lengths
carrot	1 large, cut into 1/2-inch dice
fresh or frozen peas	heaping 3/4 cup
cornichons	6, chopped
baby capers	3 tablespoons, rinsed
anchovy fillets	4, finely chopped
black olives	10, each cut into 3 slices, plus 5 extra, to garnish

mayonnaise

eggs	2 yolks, separated
Dijon mustard	1 teaspoon
extra-virgin olive oil	1/2 cup
lemon juice	3 tablespoons
garlic	2 small cloves, crushed

To make the mayonnaise, use an electric mixer to beat the egg yolks with the Dijon mustard and 1/4 teaspoon salt until creamy. Gradually add the oil in a slow, fine stream, beating constantly until all the oil has been added. Add the lemon juice, garlic, and 1 teaspoon boiling water and beat for 1 minute or until well combined. Season to taste.

Cut each artichoke heart into quarters. Rinse the potatoes, put in a saucepan, cover with salted cold water, and bring to a gentle simmer. Cook for 15–20 minutes or until tender when pierced with a knife. Drain well and allow to cool slightly. Peel and set aside. When the potatoes are completely cool, cut them into 1/2-inch dice.

Blanch the beans in boiling salted water until tender but still firm to the bite. Rinse in cold water, then drain thoroughly. Repeat with the carrot and peas.

Set aside a small quantity of each vegetable, including the chopped cornichons, for the garnish, and season to taste. Put the remainder in a bowl with the capers, anchovies, and sliced olives. Add the mayonnaise, toss to combine, and season. Arrange on a serving dish and garnish with the reserved vegetables and the whole olives.

Add the oil to the egg yolks in a slow, steady stream.

Blanch the green beans in boiling water, then refresh in cold water.

Pour the mayonnaise over the vegetables and toss to mix.

three ways with seafood tapas

A MOONLIT WANDER IN SEVILLE, PAST GARDENS AND PLAZAS FRAGRANT WITH JASMINE AND MAGNOLIA, WILL LEAD YOU TO THE TAPAS BAR QUARTER AROUND CALLE CANO Y CUETO. HERE, YOU WILL FIND THE MOST SENSATIONAL SEAFOOD TAPAS, USING SHRIMP, WHITEBAIT, AND SCALLOPS, ALL FRIED TO PERFECTION. THERE ARE ALSO DISHES OF FRIED BABY EEL, LITTLE PLATEFULS OF SWEET BABY MOLLUSKS, AND SEA SNAILS, WHICH ARE EATEN BY SUCKING THE FLESH STRAIGHT OUT OF THEIR SHELLS. THEN IT'S TIME FOR DINNER.

tortillitas de camerones

Separately sift ½ cup all-purpose flour and ½ cup chickpea flour, then combine them in a bowl. Add 1 teaspoon sweet *pimentón* (paprika) and make a well in the center. Pour in 4 lightly beaten large eggs and mix in gradually, then stir in ¼ cup water to make a smooth batter. Mix in 4 finely chopped scallions, ⅓ cup finely chopped Italian parsley, and 1 lb. 2 oz. peeled and finely chopped raw shrimp (about 1 lb. 12 oz. unpeeled) and season well. Set aside for at least 30 minutes. Heat ½ cup extra-virgin olive oil or olive oil in a deep-sided frying pan over medium-low heat. Spoon in 3 tablespoons of batter per fritter and flatten into a thin pancake. Cook in batches for about 3 minutes on each side or until golden and cooked through. Remove the fritters from the pan and drain on paper towels. Repeat with the remaining batter to make 20 in all. Season well and serve with lemon wedges. Makes 20.

calamares fritos

Wash 1 lb. 2 oz. cleaned calamari tubes and cut into rings about ½ inch thick. Combine 1½ cups all-purpose flour and 2 teaspoons sweet *pimentón* (paprika). Season the calamari rings well with salt and freshly ground black pepper and toss in the flour to lightly coat. Fill a deep, heavy-based saucepan one-third full of extra-virgin olive oil or olive oil and heat to 350°F or until a cube of bread dropped into the oil browns in 15 seconds. Add the calamari in batches and cook for about 2 minutes or until golden. Drain and serve hot with lemon wedges and allioli (page 48) on the side, if desired. Serves 4.

banderillas

Soak 8 wooden skewers in cold water for 1 hour to prevent them from burning during cooking. Cut 9 oz. good-quality raw tuna into 24 evenly sized cubes. Remove the zest from 1 lemon, avoiding the bitter white pith, and cut the zest into thin strips. Put the tuna, lemon zest, 1 tablespoon lemon juice, and 1 tablespoon olive oil in a bowl for 5–10 minutes to infuse. Using 16 capers and 8 green olives stuffed with anchovies in total, thread 3 pieces of tuna, 2 capers, and 1 green olive onto each skewer, alternating each ingredient. Put the skewers in a nonmetallic dish and pour the marinade over. Cook under a hot broiler, turning to cook each side, for about 4 minutes or until done to your liking. Makes 8.

shrimp with romesco sauce .... serves 6 to 8

THIS CLASSIC CATALAN SAUCE IS FROM THE TOWN OF TARRAGONA. IT IS BEST MADE WITH THE ROMESCO OR NYORA BELL PEPPER, THOUGH ANCHO CHILIES OR ANY DRIED BELL PEPPER WILL ALSO WORK WELL. ROMESCO SAUCE IS FAMED AS THE BASIS OF *ROMESCO DE PEIX*, THE CELEBRATED CATALAN SEAFOOD STEW.

raw large shrimp	30
olive oil	4 teaspoons

romesco sauce

garlic	4 cloves, unpeeled
plum tomato	1, halved and seeded
long red chilies	2
blanched almonds	3 tablespoons
hazelnuts	3 tablespoons
crusty white bread	2 thin slices
olive oil	for cooking
sun-dried bell peppers in oil, such as romesco or ancho	2¼ oz.
olive oil	4 teaspoons
red wine vinegar	4 teaspoons

Peel the shrimp, leaving the tails intact. Cut down the back and gently pull out the dark vein, starting at the head. Mix the shrimp with ¼ teaspoon salt and refrigerate for 30 minutes.

To make the romesco sauce, preheat the oven to 400°F. Wrap the garlic cloves in foil, put on a baking sheet with the tomato and chilies, and bake for about 12 minutes. Spread the almonds and hazelnuts on the baking sheet and bake for another 3–5 minutes. Allow to cool for 15 minutes. Fry the bread in a little olive oil, then break into rough pieces.

Transfer the almonds, hazelnuts, and fried bread pieces to a small blender or food processor and blend until finely ground. Pop the garlic out of its skin and add to the blender. Next, add the tomato to the blender. Split the chilies and remove the seeds. Scrape the flesh into the blender, discarding the skins. Pat the bell peppers dry with paper towels, then chop them and add to the blender with the olive oil, vinegar, some salt, and 3 tablespoons water. Blend until smooth, adding more water if necessary to form a soft dipping consistency. Set aside for 30 minutes.

Heat the olive oil in a frying pan over high heat and cook the shrimp for 5 minutes or until curled up and slightly pink. Serve with the romesco sauce.

Add the garlic flesh to the ground nuts and bread in the blender.

Add the remaining ingredients and blend until smooth.

calamares
a la plancha .... serves 6

A LA PLANCHA REFERS TO COOKING ON A HOT, FLAT PLATE, AS OPPOSED TO *A LA PARILLA*, WHICH IS ON A GRILL. *A LA PLANCHA* IS A FAVORITE METHOD IN MANY TAPAS BARS, AND CALAMARI PREPARED THIS WAY—SWEET AND TENDER, SLIGHTLY CHARRED, AND SPRINKLED WITH PARSLEY AND GARLIC—ARE ESPECIALLY GOOD.

small squid	1 lb. 2 oz.
olive oil	3 tablespoons

parsley dressing

extra-virgin olive oil	3 tablespoons
Italian parsley	3 tablespoons finely chopped
garlic	1 clove, crushed

To clean the squid, gently pull the tentacles away from the hood (the intestines should come away at the same time). Remove the intestines from the tentacles by cutting under the eyes, then remove the beak if it remains in the center of the tentacles by using your fingers to push up the center. Discard the beak. Pull away the soft bone from the hood.

Rub the hoods under cold running water. The skin should come away easily. Wash the hoods and tentacles, and drain well. Transfer to a bowl, add ¼ teaspoon salt, and mix well. Cover and refrigerate for 30 minutes.

Just before cooking, whisk the dressing ingredients with some salt and ¼ teaspoon freshly ground black pepper in a pitcher or bowl.

Heat the oil in a frying pan over high heat and cook the squid hoods in small batches for 2–3 minutes or until the hoods turn white and are tender. Cook the squid tentacles, turning to brown them all over, for 1 minute or until they curl up. Serve hot, drizzled with the parsley dressing.

To prepare the squid, first pull the tentacles away from the hood.

Cut under the eyes and reserve the tentacles.

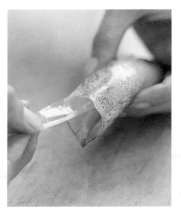

Grasp the soft bone in the hood and pull out. Discard.

Wash the squid hoods under running water, removing the skin.

allioli

"When garlic is beaten with oil and vinegar," wrote Pliny the Elder sometime in the first century AD, "it is wondrous how the foam increases." He was writing about the traditional version of this Catalan emulsion sauce, which contained only garlic—"all"—and olive oil—"oli." Garlic was crushed in a mortar with a pestle, and the olive oil added, drop by drop, until the two emulsified. A little salt, and that was it. No eggs—"allioli made with eggs," sniffed an old-fashioned Catalan, "is no allioli at all."

Be that as it may, today, because it's easier (and because the original allioli is almost unbearably garlicky), it is made with eggs. We can breathe easy.

But not too easy. Allioli should be strongly garlic in flavor and smooth and white in texture. It is the ideal sauce for seafood of all types and is perfect with potatoes and even quince (with honey stirred through it). There is another version known as drowned allioli, a kind of curdled sauce, which is stirred into fish soups and stews. Whatever kind of allioli you are making, be sure that all ingredients are at room temperature before you start. For best results use a mild, late-season extra-virgin olive oil.

Put ½ teaspoon sea salt and 4–6 garlic cloves in a mortar and gently mash to a paste with the pestle. Transfer to a food processor and add 2 egg yolks and 2 teaspoons white wine vinegar (optional). Process for several seconds. Now, using 1 cup mild extra-virgin olive oil and with the motor running, start adding the oil, drop by drop. When the mixture starts coming together, add the oil in a slow steady stream until you have a thick mayonnaise. If at some point the mayonnaise becomes too thick, add a dash of vinegar, and continue adding the oil.

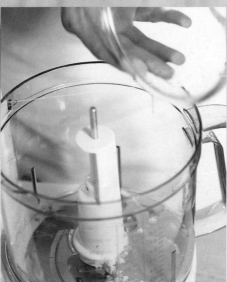

tortilla

serves 6 to 8

SUCH A SIMPLE DISH, SO DIFFICULT TO PERFECT. A TORTILLA MUST BE LIGHT, THE POTATO FIRM, THE ONIONS EVER SO SLIGHTLY CARAMELIZED, AND THE EGGS COOKED ENOUGH TO HOLD THE WHOLE THING TOGETHER BUT NO MORE. THE TORTILLA IS THE DISH BY WHICH A TAPAS BAR IS JUDGED.

potatoes	3 medium, peeled and cut into 1/2-inch slices
olive oil	1/4 cup
brown onion	1, thinly sliced
garlic	4 cloves, thinly sliced
Italian parsley	3 tablespoons finely chopped
eggs	6

Put the potato slices in a large saucepan, cover with cold water, and bring to a boil over high heat. Boil for 5 minutes, then drain and set aside.

Put the oil in a deep-sided nonstick frying pan and heat over medium heat. Add the onion and garlic, and cook for 5 minutes or until the onion softens.

Add the potatoes and parsley to the pan and stir to combine. Cook over medium heat for 5 minutes, gently pressing on the mixture.

Whisk the eggs with 1 teaspoon each of salt and freshly ground black pepper and pour evenly over the potatoes. Cover and cook over low to medium heat for 20 minutes or until the eggs are just set. Slide onto a serving plate or serve directly from the pan.

Aficionados of Spanish cooking rightly judge the tortilla to be one of the exemplars of Spain's culinary tradition of "direct and simple" cooking. Indeed it is, as well as being the subject of folk tales and a topic for argument in bars and kitchens across Spain. Nobody disagrees that its main ingredients are eggs and potatoes, but some will fight almost to the death over the inclusion or not of garlic and onions. However, all agree that it should go no further. There are other "tortillas"—a delicious one from Andalusia, called *tortilla de berenjenas*, which features eggplant—but if the recipe or menu just says tortilla, expect no more than potato—and perhaps garlic and onion.

scrambled eggs with asparagus..serves 4

CREAMY SCRAMBLED EGGS AS A STARTER? WHY NOT? THAT'S WHAT THE SPANISH CALL A *REVUELTO*: EGGS WITH FRESH SEASONAL INGREDIENTS LIKE GARLIC SHOOTS, BABY ARTICHOKES—AND ASPARAGUS.

garlic	2 cloves, chopped
bread	1 thick slice, crusts removed
olive oil	¼ cup
asparagus	1 bunch, cut into ¾-inch lengths
sweet *pimentón* (paprika)	1 teaspoon
white wine vinegar	3 tablespoons
eggs	6

Put the garlic and bread in a food processor or mortar and grind or pound to a loose paste, adding a small amount of water (1–3 tablespoons).

Heat the oil in a frying pan and sauté the asparagus over medium heat for 2 minutes or until just starting to become tender. Add the garlic paste, *pimentón*, vinegar, and a pinch of salt and stir to combine. Cover and cook over medium heat for 2–3 minutes or until the asparagus is tender.

Beat the eggs and add to the pan. Reduce the heat to low and gently fold the eggs through with a whisk or wooden fork. Remove the eggs from the heat just before they are fully cooked. Season to taste and serve immediately.

Revuelto comes from the verb *revolver*, meaning to "disturb," "mess up," "move about," or "turn over," all of which you do, gently and quickly, to make this delicious dish. The classic *revuelto* is made with the heads of *esparragos trigueros*, the tiny wild asparagus that covers the countryside in spring, or with asparagus combined with *gambas* (shrimp). In expensive restaurants, you will even find a *revuelto* of truffles in season. The trick, when making this dish, is to not overcook it, but to move the eggs constantly with a whisk or a wooden fork. Also, remove the eggs from the heat just before they are cooked—they'll continue to cook in the pan— and serve them soft and just set.

the coastline

Spain's long coastline stretches from France to Africa and is lapped by the Mediterranean Sea, the Atlantic Ocean, and the Cantabrian Sea. This geography and a history of invasions and occupations by Phoenicians, Greeks, Romans, Moors, Jews, and, last but not least, tourists, explains the wonderful variety of dishes to be found on the coast and on the Balearic Islands.

For many, Galicia, in the country's northwestern corner, is the seafood capital of Spain. Here you'll find culinary curiosities such as *percebes* (goose barnacles). These delicious morsels, eaten raw or lightly boiled, look like tiny elephant's feet and are plucked from wave-lashed rocks by intrepid gatherers. Daily fishing boats deliver to the markets fresh *langostas* and *bogavantes* (spiny lobsters and lobsters), and *buey*, the large crab named after the ox. All three are boiled in seawater by Galician cooks and served simply as a *mariscada* (seafood platter).

Similar seafood, similarly treated, is to be found all along the Cantabrian coast, but special mention must be made of the delicious *anchoas* (anchovies) of the Basque country, which are usually washed down with *chacoli*, the crisp white wine of Guetaria, which comes from vines grown on the slopes overlooking the sea.

In winter, all along the Spanish Atlantic coast, in estuaries and the mouths of rivers, wherever eels spawn, *angulas* (baby eels) are caught. This expensive luxury is usually fried with garlic and dried bell peppers, a dish known as *angulas a la bilbaina* (Bilbao-style baby eels). But if we move into Catalonia and the Mediterranean, we'll find an altogether different kettle of fish on offer. Here, besides the elaborate Catalan seafood stew *zarzuela*, Catalans love *calamares a la plancha* (grilled calamari), *salmonetes al horno* (baked red mullet), or *una parillada de mariscos* (mixed grill of fish and/or shellfish).

Finally, in the southernmost province of Andalusia, you will find exquisitely fried fish being eaten in *freidurías* (stores specializing in frying). Andalusian frying is famed and the secret to the technique lies in large quantities of hot olive oil. Try *filetes de merluza* (hake steaks), *acedías* (wedge sole), fans of anchovies tied by the tail, or *cazón* (dogfish) marinated in vinegar, garlic, and cumin, then fried.

Besides seafood, the other great coastal ingredient is rice. First introduced by the Moors, rice has been cultivated continually in coastal wetlands and river valleys and is used in hundreds of dishes around the coast, the most famous of which is paella—which has become, without question—Spain's national dish.

pulpo gallego .... serves 4

MELT-IN-THE-MOUTH OCTOPUS, RED WITH *PIMENTÓN* AND GLISTENING WITH EXTRA-VIRGIN OLIVE OIL, MAKES *PULPO GALLEGO* A LONG-STANDING FAVORITE IN TAPAS BARS. IT IS USUALLY SERVED ON A WOODEN PLATTER, FRESH OFF THE GRILL. FOR COMPLETE ENJOYMENT, SERVE WITH A GALICIAN *RIBEIRO* OR SIMILAR YOUNG WINE.

octopuses	2, weighing approximately 1 lb. 2 oz. each
bay leaf	1
black peppercorns	10
smoked or sweet *pimentón* (paprika)	for sprinkling
extra-virgin olive oil	3 tablespoons
lemon wedges	to serve

Wash the octopuses. Using a sharp knife, carefully cut between the head and tentacles of the octopus, just below the eyes. Grasp the body of the octopus and push the beak up and out through the center of the tentacles with your fingers. Discard. Cut the eyes from the head of the octopus by slicing the small disk off with a sharp knife. Discard the eye section.

To clean the octopus head, carefully slit through one side (taking care not to break the ink sac) and scrape out any guts from inside. Rinse under running water to remove any remaining guts.

Bring a large saucepan of water to a boil. Add the bay leaf, peppercorns, 1 teaspoon salt, and the octopus pieces. Reduce the heat and simmer for 1 hour or until tender.

Remove the octopus pieces from the water, drain well, and set aside for about 10 minutes.

Cut the tentacles into ½-inch-thick slices and cut the head into bite-sized pieces. Arrange on a serving platter and sprinkle with *pimentón* and salt. Drizzle with the extra-virgin olive oil and garnish with lemon wedges.

To prepare the octopus, first cut the head from the tentacles.

Remove the beak by pushing it up and out through the tentacles.

Cut the small disk—the eye—away from the head and discard.

Carefully scrape away the guts from the head and discard.

bacalao with red bell pepper .... serves 6

CERTAIN COMBINATIONS OF INGREDIENTS JUST NATURALLY WORK WELL TOGETHER. ONE SUCH COMBINATION IS THAT OF *BACALAO* (SALT COD) WITH SWEET RED BELL PEPPER AND TOMATOES, AS THIS DISH HAPPILY PROVES. IT IS FOUND, IN VARIOUS FORMS, ON TABLES THROUGHOUT SPAIN.

bacalao (salt cod)	14 oz.
red bell pepper	1
olive oil	4 teaspoons
onion	1 small, chopped
garlic	1 clove, crushed
chili flakes	1/4 teaspoon
sweet *pimentón* (paprika)	1 teaspoon
dry white wine	1/4 cup
vine-ripened tomatoes	2, finely chopped
tomato paste	4 teaspoons
Italian parsley	4 teaspoons chopped

Soak the bacalao in plenty of cold water for 20 hours, changing the water four or five times to remove excess saltiness. Add the fish to a saucepan of boiling water, reduce the heat—it should be no more than 150°F—and gently poach for 35–45 minutes. Drain and leave until cool. Remove the skin and flake the fish into large pieces, removing any bones. Put in a bowl.

Preheat the broiler. Cut the bell pepper into quarters, remove the seeds, and broil, skin side up, until the skin blackens and blisters. Cool in a plastic bag, then peel. Slice thinly.

Heat the oil in a saucepan over medium heat, add the onion, and cook, stirring occasionally, for 3 minutes or until translucent. Add the garlic, chili, and *pimentón* and cook for 1 minute. Increase the heat to high, add the white wine, and simmer for 30 seconds. Reduce the heat, add the tomatoes and tomato paste, and cook, stirring occasionally, for 5 minutes or until thick. Add the fish, cover, and simmer for about 5 minutes. Add the bell pepper and parsley and taste before seasoning with salt. Serve hot.

There are almost as many Basque recipes for *bacalao* as there used to be cod in the waters of the North Atlantic. The most famous of these recipes is *bacalao pil pil*, which is, quite simply, salt cod in a rich and creamy emulsion of olive oil and garlic. This receipe, an example of the many that team salt cod with a red bell pepper and tomatoes, works wonders by balancing the sweetness of the bell pepper and the acidity of the tomatoes with the texture and slight residual saltiness of the fish. *Bacalao* also works well with *pimentón*, garlic, onion, and eggplant. This dish is a variation on the many that probably originated in the Vizcaya region, whose capital is Bilbao.

bacalao

Over a thousand years ago, Basque fishermen regularly set off from the coast of northern Spain for Newfoundland, off the eastern coast of Canada, a distance of some 2,800 miles. Their original quarry was the whale, whale meat being a delicacy in medieval times. But soon they became aware of a fishery so vast that it was said you could step off a boat and walk across the water on the backs of the fish swarming the icy waters. The fish were Atlantic cod (*Gadus morhua*).

The cod were transported to the markets of Europe just as whale meat was—salted and dried where it was caught. The result, *bacalao*, became a staple of the Spanish and Portuguese table for Lent, an answer to devout Catholic prayers for an economical fish for the Friday abstention meal. However, in 1992, after a millennium of exploitation, the vast fisheries off Newfoundland collapsed and have yet to recover. *Bacalao*, now from Norway, is no longer a cheap staple, but a luxury for connoisseurs.

Why eat *bacalao* when fresh fish is so readily available? Why eat ham when you can eat pork? It is a separate product, much loved for its unique flavor and texture and for the dishes that have evolved around it.

Cooking *bacalao* is not a straightforward process. First, you must choose a well-cured piece (avoid the cheaper but inferior product made from ling fish). Good *bacalao* has white, flexible meat, dark skin, and a unique smell; the best cuts tend to appear at Easter. But before you cook your *bacalao*, you must prepare it. There are two ways to do this. One is to grill it over coals until it becomes soft and damp. It is then easy to remove the bones and skin and to rinse the flesh in water to remove excess salt. The second way, the time-honored method, is to submerge the fish in fresh water for 20 hours, changing the water four or five times, then to poach it in water no hotter than 150°F for 35–45 minutes. This is also a good test of the quality of your *bacalao*. If it is of poor quality, it will collapse into a fibrous mass. If it is of good quality, it will emerge smooth, firm, and white—and without the oversalted flavor of badly cooked *bacalao* dishes.

sardinas murcianas

ALL ALONG THE MURCIAN COAST, IN SPAIN'S SOUTHEAST, SARDINES ARE LANDED AND TRANSPORTED, STILL FLAPPING, TO KITCHENS ALONG THE SEAFRONT. WITH SEAFOOD, FRESHNESS IS EVERYTHING, BUT THIS IS ESPECIALLY SO FOR SPAIN'S MUCH-LOVED *SARDINA*.

vine-ripened tomatoes	8 medium
fresh large sardines	24, cleaned, with backbones, heads, and tails removed
green bell peppers	2, seeded and cut into thin rings
onion	1, sliced into thin rings
potatoes	2, cut into ¼-inch-thick slices
Italian parsley	3 tablespoons chopped, plus extra, to garnish
garlic	3 cloves, crushed
saffron threads	¼ teaspoon, lightly roasted
olive oil	3 tablespoons

Score a cross in the base of each tomato. Put in a bowl of boiling water for 10 seconds, then plunge into cold water and peel away the skin from the cross. Cut each tomato into thin slices.

Preheat the oven to 350°F. Lightly oil a large, shallow, earthenware or ceramic baking dish wide enough to hold the sardines. On a wooden board or clean work surface, gently open out the sardines and lightly sprinkle the insides with salt. Fold them back into their original shape.

Cover the base of the baking dish with a third of the tomatoes. Layer half the sardines on top. Follow with a layer of half the belll peppers, then half the onion, then half the potatoes. Sprinkle with half the parsley and garlic, and season with freshly ground black pepper. Crumble half the saffron over the top.

Layer the remaining sardines, half the remaining tomatoes, and then the other ingredients as before. Finish with the last of the tomatoes. Season well with salt and freshly ground black pepper. Drizzle the olive oil over the surface and cover with foil. Bake for 1 hour or until the potatoes are cooked. Spoon off any excess liquid, sprinkle with extra parsley, and serve straight from the dish.

Gently open the sardines out and sprinkle with salt.

Fill a dish with alternate layers of filling and sardine, then cook.

octopus in garlic almond sauce . . . . serves 4

THIS IS A MODERN RECIPE, COMBINING CLASSIC INGREDIENTS FROM THE OLD WORLD—OCTOPUS, GARLIC, AND ALMONDS—WITH A CLASSIC INGREDIENT FROM THE NEW: RED BELL PEPPER. THE RESULT: A MARRIAGE OF WONDERFUL FLAVOR AND TEXTURE.

baby octopuses	2 lb. 4 oz.
red bell pepper	½ small, seeded
flaked almonds	1⅓ cups
garlic	3 cloves, crushed
red wine vinegar	⅓ cup
olive oil	¾ cup
Italian parsley	3 tablespoons chopped

Using a small knife, carefully cut between the head and tentacles of each of the octopuses and use your fingers to push the beak up and out through the center of the tentacles. Discard. To clean the octopus head, carefully slit through one side and pull out or chop out the gut. Rinse under running water. Drop the octopus pieces into a large saucepan of boiling water and simmer for 20–40 minutes, depending on their size, until tender. (After 15 minutes, start pricking the octopus with a skewer to test for tenderness.) When cooked, remove the pan from the heat and cool the octopus in the water for 15 minutes.

To make the sauce, heat the broiler to high. Broil the bell pepper, skin side up, until the skin blackens and blisters all over. Cool in a plastic bag. Peel away the skin, put the pepper in a food processor with the almonds and garlic, and purée. With the motor running, gradually add the vinegar followed by the oil. Stir in ½ cup boiling water and the parsley, and season to taste with salt and freshly ground black pepper.

To serve, cut the tentacles into pieces. Put all the octopus pieces in a serving bowl with the sauce and toss to coat. Serve warm, or chill and serve as a light salad.

First cut the head away from the tentacles, then remove the beak.

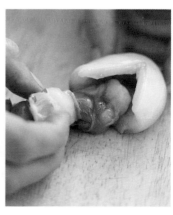

Pull out the gut from the head and wash the head.

Remove the eye by simply slicing away the small disk on the head.

three ways with seafood and wine

THE GRAPES GROWN AND HARVESTED ALONG SPANISH COASTLINES AND RIVER BANKS OFTEN RETURN, AS WINE, TO BE UNITED WITH THE SEAFOOD PLUCKED FROM THAT SAME COAST OR RIVER, EITHER IN THE PREPARATION OF DISHES OR AS AN ACCOMPANIMENT TO THEIR EATING. A CHILLED *ROSADO* (ROSÉ) WITH *CALAMARES A LA PLANCHA* AT A BEACHSIDE RESTAURANT, A SPLASH OF WHITE WINE INTO A PAN OF SAUTÉED MUSSELS, OR A DASH OF *FINO* SHERRY INTO A COOKING POT CONTAINING FRESH CLAMS ARE JUST A FEW WAYS THE TWO CAN BE UNITED.

scallops with *cava* sauce

Remove and discard the vein, membrane, or hard white muscle from 20 large white scallops. Remove the roe. Melt 4 tablespoons butter in a large heavy-based frying pan over medium-high heat. Sauté the scallops for 1–2 minutes on each side or until almost cooked through. Transfer to a plate. Add 3 tablespoons thinly sliced French shallots to the pan and cook for 3 minutes or until soft. Add 1½ cups *cava* or other sparkling wine and simmer for 6–8 minutes or until reduced by half. Stir in 1 cup light cream and simmer for about 10 minutes or until the liquid is reduced to a sauce consistency. Stir in 2–3 teaspoons lemon juice and season with salt and pepper. Return the scallops to the sauce to reheat gently, then serve garnished with 4 teaspoons chopped Italian parsley. Serves 4.

clams in fino sherry

Soak 2 lb. 4 oz. clams in salted water for 1 hour to release any grit. Rinse under running water and discard any open clams. Heat 3 tablespoons extra-virgin olive oil in a heavy saucepan, then add 2 finely chopped garlic cloves and fry until lightly golden. Add ½ cup fino sherry and 3 tablespoons chopped Italian parsley, and season lightly. Add the clams and cook, covered, for about 4 minutes, shaking the pan vigorously a few times. Discard any clams that do not open. Serve the rest, with the sauce, hot or cold. Serves 4.

sherry with oysters

Not so much a recipe as a revelation. First, shuck your live oysters using a sharp oyster knife. To do this, wrap a dish towel around your hand and use that hand to hold the first oyster, rounded side down. Insert the knife between the two shells, near the hinge. Twist the knife to separate the shells; this will sever the muscle that connects the oyster to the shell. Slide the knife blade underneath the oyster to detach it from the shell. Repeat with the remaining oysters (if unsure, ask your fish dealer for a lesson). Put the oysters on a bed of ice and eat, with no accompaniments (a squeeze of lemon juice if you must) except a glass of chilled fino or manzanilla sherry. This marriage of freshly shucked oysters and chilled dry sherry is a perfect match of texture, flavor, and weight. Allow 4–6 oysters per person.

clams with white wine .... serves 4

WHAT COULD BE SIMPLER AND MORE DELICIOUS THAN FRESH CLAMS STEAMED OPEN IN WHITE WINE AND GARLIC, THE FLAVORS MINGLING WITH THE CLAM'S OWN JUICES OF THE SEA.

clams	2 lb. 4 oz.
vine-ripened tomatoes	2 large
olive oil	3 tablespoons
onion	1 small, finely chopped
garlic	2 cloves, crushed
Italian parsley	4 teaspoons chopped
nutmeg	a pinch
dry white wine	1/3 cup

Soak the clams in salted water for 1 hour to release any grit. Rinse under running water and discard any open clams.

Score a cross in the base of each tomato. Place in a bowl of boiling water for 10 seconds, then plunge into cold water and peel away the skin from the cross. Cut the tomatoes in half and scoop out the seeds with a teaspoon. Finely chop the tomatoes.

Heat the oil in a large flameproof casserole dish and cook the onion over low heat for 5 minutes or until softened. Add the garlic and tomatoes and cook for 5 minutes. Add the parsley and nutmeg and season with salt and pepper. Add 1/3 cup water.

Add the clams and cook, covered, over low heat until they open (discard any that do not open). Add the wine and cook over low heat for 3–4 minutes or until the sauce thickens, gently moving the casserole dish back and forth a few times, rather than stirring, so that the clams stay in the shells. Serve immediately, with bread.

The surrounding seas deliver a variety of clams onto Spanish tables, most often the *almeja* (carpet shell), but also the *coquina* (wedge shell), *berberecho* (cockle), and the curious-looking *navaja* (razor clam), which does indeed resemble an old-fashioned razor blade. Clams are treated simply in Spanish cooking: they are steamed open and eaten; thrown on a charbroil pan; or tossed into a simple steaming broth, such as here, and flavored with ingredients like wine, garlic, and tomatoes. On the Catalan coast, where pasta is common, the little town of Gandía makes a dish that combines clams with the short, thin pasta *fideus*.

rice with
stuffed squid .... serves 4

THIS IS ANOTHER EXAMPLE OF THE GLORIOUS RICE DISHES TO BE FOUND IN SPAIN. HERE, SHORT-GRAINED RICE
IS TEAMED WITH SWEET, PLUMP LITTLE SQUID STUFFED WITH CURRANTS AND PINE NUTS.

small squid	8
onion	1 small
olive oil	3 tablespoons
currants	3 tablespoons
pine nuts	3 tablespoons
fresh breadcrumbs	1/3 cup
mint	4 teaspoons chopped
Italian parsley	4 teaspoons chopped
egg	1, lightly beaten
all-purpose flour	2 teaspoons

sauce

olive oil	4 teaspoons
onion	1 small, finely chopped
garlic	1 clove, crushed
dry white wine	1/4 cup
chopped tomatoes	14-oz. can
sugar	1/2 teaspoon
bay leaf	1

rice

fish stock	5 cups
olive oil	1/4 cup
onion	1, finely chopped
garlic	3 cloves, crushed
short-grain rice	1 1/4 cups
cayenne pepper	1/4 teaspoon
squid ink	1 tablespoon (saved from the squid above or bought separately)
dry white wine	1/4 cup
tomato paste	1/4 cup
Italian parsley	3 tablespoons chopped

To clean the squid, gently pull the tentacles away from the hood (the intestines should come away at the same time). Reserve the ink sac, if using in this recipe. Remove the intestines from the tentacles by cutting under the eyes, then remove the beak if it remains in the center of the tentacles by using your fingers to push up the center. Discard the beak. Pull away the soft bone from the hood.

Rub the hoods under cold running water. The skin should come away easily. Wash the hoods and tentacles and drain well.

Put the tentacles and onion in a processor and finely chop. Heat the oil in a saucepan and cook the currants and pine nuts over low heat until lightly browned. Remove from the pan. Add the onion mixture, cook gently for 5 minutes, and then add to the pine-nut mixture with the breadcrumbs, herbs, and egg. Season. Stuff into the squid hoods, close the openings, and secure with toothpicks. Dust with flour.

To make the sauce, heat the oil in a frying pan and cook the onion over low heat for 5 minutes or until soft. Stir in the garlic, wine, and 1/2 cup water. Cook over high heat for 1 minute, then add the tomatoes, sugar, and bay leaf. Season, reduce the heat, and simmer for 5 minutes. Add the squid to the pan in a single layer. Simmer, covered, for 20 minutes or until tender.

To make the rice, bring the stock to a simmer in a saucepan. Heat the oil in a saucepan and cook the onion over low heat until soft. Add the garlic, rice, and cayenne pepper. Mix the squid ink with 1/3 cup of the stock, add to the rice with the wine and tomato paste, and stir until the liquid has almost evaporated. Add 1 cup stock, simmer until this evaporates, and then add the remaining stock, 1 cup at a time, until the rice is tender and creamy. Cover and remove from the heat for about 5 minutes. Season and stir in the parsley. Put the rice on a serving plate, arrange the squid on top, and spoon over the sauce.

three ways with tuna

"THREE THOUSAND WAYS WITH TUNA" WOULD BE JUST AS FEASIBLE FOR THIS FIRM-FLESHED AND FULL-BODIED FISH. TUNA HAS BEEN ENJOYED AND EATEN ALL AROUND THE MEDITERRANEAN SINCE TIME IMMEMORIAL. FRESH TUNA, EITHER *ATÚN* (BLUE FIN), *ALBACORA* (ALBACORE), *BACORETA* (LITTLE TUNA), OR *LISTADO* (SKIPJACK), IS OFTEN SIMPLY BARBECUED OR CHARBROILED, SPRINKLED WITH LEMON JUICE, AND TOPPED WITH PARSLEY AND FRIED GARLIC. YOU WILL ALSO SEE CANNED TUNA IN OLIVE OIL SERVED ON *BOCADILLOS* (BREAD ROLLS).

marmitako

Preheat the oven to 350°F. Heat 3 tablespoons olive oil in a saucepan over medium heat and add 1 diced onion, 1 seeded and roughly diced red bell pepper, and 2 teaspoons sweet *pimentón* (paprika). Cook for 3 minutes or until soft. Add another tablespoon oil if necessary, then add 2 finely chopped garlic cloves, 2 bay leaves, and 1 cup canned chopped tomatoes, and cook for 10 minutes. Add 1/3 cup white wine and 1/4 cup drained capers and stir through. Peel 4 medium potatoes and cut into 1/2-inch-thick slices. Arrange the potato slices in the bottom of a shallow 10 1/2 x 8-inch casserole or heatproof dish. Evenly spread the tomato and onion mixture over the potato and pour 1 cup chicken stock over. Bake for 40 minutes or until the potato is almost cooked. Season 4 x 7-oz. tuna steaks with salt and freshly ground black pepper and arrange on top of the potato. Bake for 5–8 minutes for rare or 10–15 minutes for medium. Season well and sprinkle 1 handful chopped Italian parsley, 1 tablespoon lemon juice, and 1 seeded and finely chopped small red chili (optional) over the top before serving. Serves 4.

tuna with tomato sauce

Combine 4 x 7-oz. tuna steaks with 1/3 cup lemon juice, 4 teaspoons chopped Italian parsley, and a large pinch of salt, and allow to marinate for 15 minutes. Preheat the oven to 350°F. Heat 1/3 cup oil in a saucepan over medium heat and cook 1 finely chopped onion and 2 chopped garlic cloves for 5 minutes or until translucent. Add 14-oz. can tomatoes, 1 bay leaf, 1 teaspoon sugar, 1 teaspoon chopped thyme, and 4 teaspoons chopped Italian parsley, and season to taste. Increase the heat to high and cook for 3 minutes or until some of the liquid has reduced. Heat 1/3 cup oil in a large frying pan over medium-high heat. Drain the tuna steaks and coat in all-purpose flour. Cook for about 3 minutes on each side or until golden, then transfer to a large casserole dish. Cover the tuna with the tomato sauce, and bake for 20 minutes or until the tuna flakes easily. Serves 4.

braised tuna

Flour and salt a thick piece of fresh tuna (1 lb. 2 oz.). Add 1/3 cup extra-virgin olive oil to a deep flameproof casserole dish and set over medium heat. When the oil is hot, add the tuna. Turn it several times until it is browned all over. Add 1 sliced onion, 2 chopped tomatoes, 2 finely chopped garlic cloves, 1 bay leaf, and 2/3 cup white wine. Reduce the heat to low, cover, and leave for 30–50 minutes or until the tuna is thoroughly cooked. Remove the tuna from the dish, allow to cool, and then cut into slices. Pass the sauce through a fine strainer and return to the dish. Reheat, then pour over the tuna. Serve with a green salad. Serves 4.

trout with *jamón* . . . . serves 4

THE COLD MOUNTAIN RIVERS OF NAVARRA TEEM WITH TROUT, WHICH ARE CAUGHT FOR SPORT AND FOOD. THIS RECIPE, OFTEN CALLED *TRUCHA A LA NAVARRA*, USES BACON FAT AS THE COOKING MEDIUM (OLIVE OIL WAS ONCE AN EXPENSIVE LUXURY FOR THE NAVARRA COOKS.) SERVE THIS DISH WITH A ROSÉ FROM THE AREA.

river trout	4 x 7 oz., cleaned and deboned
mint	1 bunch, broken into sprigs
white wine	³⁄4 cup
jamón or prosciutto	8 slices
bacon fat or olive oil	3 tablespoons
lemon juice	3 tablespoons
butter	3 tablespoons, cold, chopped

Stuff each trout cavity with several sprigs of mint. Arrange in a dish in which they fit together snugly and drizzle with the wine. Cover and marinate in the refrigerator for at least 6 hours.

Preheat the oven to 350°F. Remove the fish from the marinade and pat dry, reserving the marinade. Remove the mint from each trout cavity and discard. Season the cavity. Roll up two pieces of *jamón* per fish and put in the cavity with some more mint sprigs.

Heat the bacon fat in a large frying pan over medium heat for 4 minutes or until melted. Add the fish and fry for 3 minutes on each side or until crisp. Transfer the fish to an ovenproof dish and bake for 10 minutes or until the fish is no longer translucent and can be flaked easily with a fork.

Meanwhile, combine the reserved marinade and lemon juice in the frying pan and boil over high heat for about 5 minutes or until the sauce reduces to a syrupy consistency. Gradually whisk in the butter until the sauce is slightly shiny. Serve the fish with the *jamón* and mint inside, drizzled with the sauce.

Fill the cavity of each trout with *jamón* and fresh mint.

Gently fry the filled trout, in batches if necessary, until crisp.

Add the butter to the sauce, whisking until it turns shiny.

baked bream with bell pepper, chili, and potatoes

.... serves 4 to 6

WHO SAID FISH CAN'T MAKE A HEARTY MEAL? YOU WILL OFTEN FIND SATISFYING DISHES LIKE THIS ONE MARRYING FISH (SUCH AS HAKE AND *BACALAO*) WITH POTATOES, ESPECIALLY IN COLD AND ARID NORTHERN SPAIN.

whole red bream, red snapper or porgy	2 lb. 12 oz., cleaned
lemon	1
olive oil	¼ cup
potatoes	5 medium, thinly sliced
garlic	3 cloves, thinly sliced
Italian parsley	¼ cup finely chopped
red onion	1 small, thinly sliced
dried chili	1 small, seeded and finely chopped
red bell pepper	1, seeded and cut into thin rings
yellow bell pepper	1, seeded and cut into thin rings
bay leaves	2
thyme	3–4 sprigs
dry sherry	¼ cup

Cut off and discard the fins from the fish and put it in a large, nonmetallic dish. Cut 2 thin slices from the middle of the lemon and reserve. Squeeze the juice from the rest of the lemon into the cavity of the fish. Add 3 tablespoons of the oil and refrigerate, covered, for 2 hours.

Preheat the oven to 375°F and lightly oil a shallow earthenware baking dish large enough to hold the whole fish. Spread half the potato slices on the base and sprinkle with the garlic, parsley, onion, chili, and bell pepper. Season with salt and freshly ground black pepper. Cover with the rest of the potato. Pour in ⅓ cup water and sprinkle the remaining olive oil over the top. Cover with foil and bake for 1 hour.

Increase the oven temperature to 425°F. Season the fish inside and out with salt and pepper and put the bay leaves and thyme inside the cavity. Make 3 or 4 diagonal slashes on each side. Cut the reserved lemon slices in half. Nestle the fish on the potatoes and fit the lemon slices into the slashes on the top side of the fish to resemble fins. Bake, uncovered, for about 30 minutes or until the fish is cooked through and the potatoes are golden and crusty.

Pour the sherry over the fish and return to the oven for 3 minutes. Serve straight from the dish.

Lay the vegetables and spices in a dish, with half the potatoes on top.

Add the fish to the dish, fitting the lemon slices into its flesh.

three ways with salt

SPANISH FOOD IS SALTY. SALT IS USED UNSPARINGLY IN ALL SORTS OF FOOD PREPARATION: FOR EXAMPLE, WHERE ITALIANS CURE PROSCIUTTO BY RUBBING A LEG OF PORK WITH SALT, THE SPANISH BURY THEIRS IN SALT. LIKEWISE IN COOKING: SALT IS NOT SPARED WHEN MAKING *COCIDOS* (STEWS), RICE DISHES, OR SOUPS. NO CONVINCING EXPLANATIONS ARE OFFERED FOR THIS STRANGE ADDICTION. WE CAN ONLY CONJECTURE THAT IT IS DUE TO THE EXCELLENCE AND ABUNDANCE OF SPANISH SALT, ESPECIALLY THE MINERAL-RICH SEA SALTS.

fish baked in salt

Preheat the oven to 400°F. Rinse 4 lb. scaled and cleaned whole fish (such as blue-eye, jewfish, sea bass, groper), and pat dry inside and out with paper towels. Slice 2 lemons and put the slices into the fish cavity, along with 4 thyme sprigs and 1 thinly sliced fennel bulb. Pack 3 lb. 5 oz. rock salt into a large baking dish and put the fish on top. Cover with the same amount of salt again, pressing down until the salt is packed firmly around the fish. Bake the fish for 30–40 minutes or until a skewer inserted into the center of the fish comes out hot. Carefully remove the salt from the top of the fish and move to one side of the dish. Carefully peel the skin away, ensuring that no salt remains on the flesh. Serve hot or cold with allioli (page 48) or your choice of accompaniment. Serves 4–6.

shrimp boiled in seawater

If you have access to clean seawater, collect 12 cups of it, allow to stand for 1 hour, and then carefully pour the water into a large saucepan, leaving behind any sediment. Fill a second large saucepan with water and plenty of ice. Bring the seawater to a rolling boil and add 2 lb. 4 oz. unshelled green shrimp. Cook for 3 minutes, then scoop the shrimp out and plunge them into the iced water for 1 minute. Scoop out and serve (shelled or unshelled), with allioli (page 48) on the side. (If you don't have access to clean seawater, cook the shrimp in exactly the same way in water in which you have dissolved 1/4 cup sea salt.) Serves 4.

anchovies on toast

Salted anchovies in olive oil are one of the great Spanish export products. The following is a popular Spanish snack. You will need to allow 2 anchovies, 2 strips marinated bell pepper (page 31), 2 pitted black olives, and 1 slice crusty bread per person. Using a toothpick, fix the anchovies, strips of bell pepper, and black olives to a slice of crusty bread, then submerge the bread in a saucepan of very hot olive oil. Remove when the bread is golden brown, drain on paper towels, and serve.

escabeche . . . . serves 4

THIS ANCIENT AND CURIOUS METHOD OF PREPARING AND PRESERVING FISH IS ALSO A DELICIOUSLY SWEET, SOUR, AND SPICY DISH. THIS RECIPE IS A MODERN VARIATION ON THE BASIC *ESCABECHE*, AS IT USES ORANGE JUICE AND ZEST, BORROWED FROM THE SOUTH AMERICAN SEVICHE, ITSELF AN ADAPTATION OF *ESCABECHE*.

all-purpose flour	for dusting
skinless fish fillets, such as red mullet, whiting, redfish, garfish	1 lb. 2 oz.
extra-virgin olive oil	3 tablespoons, plus 1/4 cup, extra
red onion	1, thinly sliced
garlic	2 cloves, thinly sliced
thyme	2 sprigs
ground cumin	1 teaspoon
scallions	2, finely chopped
orange zest	1/2 teaspoon finely grated
orange juice	1/4 cup
white wine	3/4 cup
white wine vinegar	3/4 cup
pitted green olives	2 1/4 oz., roughly chopped
superfine sugar	1/2 teaspoon

Mix a little salt and freshly ground black pepper into the flour and lightly dust the fish with the flour. Heat the oil in a frying pan over medium heat and add the fish in batches. Cook the fish on both sides until lightly browned and just cooked through (the fish should flake easily when tested with a fork). Remove the fish from the pan and put in a single, flat layer in a large, shallow nonmetallic dish.

Heat the remaining oil in the same pan, add the onion and garlic, and cook, stirring, over medium heat for 5 minutes or until soft.

Add the thyme, cumin, and scallions and stir until fragrant. Add the orange zest, orange juice, wine, vinegar, olives, sugar, and freshly ground black pepper, to taste. Bring to a boil and pour over the fish. Allow to cool in the liquid, then refrigerate overnight. Serve at room temperature.

Escabeche is both the name of the dish and a form of preserving fish. It involves frying, then marinating fish, a method that has survived, almost intact, since Roman times. The Roman Apicius (*c.* 80 BC–AD 40), whose recipes survive in fragments, records a dish of fried fish sprinkled with hot vinegar. The word *escabeche* comes down to us from the Arabic language of medieval times, and the technique was also embellished by the cooks of that period. Apart from the Latin American seviche, *escabeche* has also migrated to many European countries. Today, this method of imparting a sweet-sour flavor to food is used with meat, vegetables, and poultry.

skate with sherry vinegar .... serves 4

THE MEDITERRANEAN IS ALIVE WITH LAZILY FLAPPING RAYS AND SKATES, FROM WHOSE WINGS THIS DELICACY IS HARVESTED. HERE IT IS TEAMED WITH ANOTHER FAVORITE SPANISH INGREDIENT, SHERRY VINEGAR.

sherry vinegar	½ cup
olive oil	⅓ cup
garlic	6 cloves, crushed
dried red chili	1 small, seeded and chopped
Italian parsley	3 tablespoons chopped
sweet *pimentón* (paprika)	1 teaspoon
saffron threads	¼ teaspoon
dried oregano	1 teaspoon
vegetable oil	⅓ cup
brown onion	1, chopped
leek	1, chopped
skate fillets	4 x 7 oz.
lemon wedges	to serve, optional

Put the vinegar in a saucepan over high heat and bring to a boil. Boil for 3 minutes or until reduced by half. Leave to cool, then add the olive oil, half the garlic, the chopped chili, and some salt. Meanwhile, combine the parsley, *pimentón*, saffron threads, and oregano in a mortar or food processor and process to a paste.

Heat 3 tablespoons of the vegetable oil in a frying pan over medium heat and cook the spice paste, onion, leek, and remaining garlic for 5 minutes or until the onion and leek are translucent. Remove from the frying pan and set aside.

Add the remaining oil to the pan, add the skate in batches, and brown each side for 4–5 minutes, depending on the thickness of the fillets. Remove and cover with foil to keep warm. Return the onion and leek mixture to the frying pan and heat through.

Drizzle the dressing over the fish and spoon on the onion and leek mixture. Garnish with lemon wedges, if using.

The wing flaps from the ray and skate are a Mediterranean delicacy often avoided by English-speaking cooks. However, there is no reason not to try them. The long strands of flesh found on the wings are delicious and well worth the effort of getting to know the fish. Like shark and dogfish, ray and skate have cartilage rather than bones. Do not be put off by a slight smell of ammonia to the flesh when you buy it—this indicates health (a complex matter of the body chemistry of nonbony fish) and will disappear during cooking. For the same reason, it's best not to eat ray or skate too fresh—a day or two of aging improves the flesh.

three ways with fish sauces

HERE ARE THREE ANCIENT DISHES COMBINING SEAFOOD WITH SAUCE: A TWELFTH-CENTURY CATALAN *JURVERT* OR *JOLIVERT*—THAT IS, GREEN SAUCE—MODERNIZED AS SALSA VERDE AND SERVED WITH THAT MOST SPANISH OF FISH, *MERLUZA* (HAKE); AN UPDATED VERSION OF A MOORISH DISH OF SALMON IN ORANGE SAUCE; AND A MODERN VERSION OF A TRADITIONAL ASTURIAN FISHERMEN'S RECIPE FOR *BOGAVANTE* (LOBSTER). ALL THREE ARE EASY TO COOK AND WONDERFUL TO EAT IN THE TWENTY-FIRST CENTURY.

hake in green sauce

Dust 4 x 7-oz. hake steaks (or use gem fish) with seasoned flour, shaking off any excess. Heat $\frac{1}{3}$ cup olive oil in a large frying pan over medium heat and add 3 chopped garlic cloves and 2 seeded and chopped green chilies. Cook for 1 minute or until the garlic just starts to brown. Remove the garlic and chili with a slotted spoon. Increase the heat to high and cook the hake for about 1 minute on each side. Remove from the pan. Add $\frac{1}{2}$ cup white wine, $\frac{2}{3}$ cup fish stock, 3 tablespoons chopped Italian parsley, and the garlic and chili mixture to the pan and simmer until the sauce has thickened to your liking. Lightly blanch 12 asparagus spears and cut into $1\frac{1}{2}$-inch lengths. Add the aparagus, the fish, $\frac{1}{2}$ cup cooked green peas, and 1 handful chopped parsley to the pan and simmer until the fish is cooked through. Serve immediately. Serves 4.

andalusian salmon in orange sauce

Finely julienne the pith-free zest of 4 Valencia oranges (or, better still, if you can get them, the bitter oranges from Seville) and squeeze their juice. Set both aside. Put $\frac{1}{4}$ cup extra-virgin olive oil and 2 finely chopped onions in a large, nonreactive saucepan over medium heat and fry for 10 minutes, stirring frequently. Cut a skinless piece of salmon fillet weighing 2 lb. 12 oz. into 8 strips, then lightly flour the strips. Add the fish to the pan and cook with the onions for about 5 minutes, shaking the pan. Add the reserved orange juice, 4 teaspoons white wine vinegar, 3 tablespoons sugar, and 1 cup fish stock, and cook for about 8 minutes over medium heat. Add the reserved julienned zest and cook, uncovered, until the sauce is syrupy and the fish is tender. Season and serve. Serves 4.

lobster in *pimentón* sauce

Buy 1 live rock lobster or lobster weighing 3 lb. 5 oz. or 2 smaller crawfish. Freeze for about 2 hours, then plunge into boiling water. Cut the lobster or crawfish into claws and $\frac{3}{4}$-inch rounds, conserving the mustard (contents of the head) and juices. If unsure, ask your fish dealer to do this for you. Put $\frac{1}{2}$ cup olive oil in a large, nonreactive saucepan. Add 2 finely chopped onions, 1 whole red chilli, and 1 tablespoon sweet *pimentón* (paprika) and fry over medium heat for 3 minutes. Add $\frac{2}{3}$ –1 cup fino sherry and let the alcohol cook off, taking care not to burn the *pimentón*. Add the lobster or crawfish pieces, with the mustard and juices, and cook, uncovered, for 10–15 minutes over medium-low heat, or until the flesh is cooked and opaque. Put $2\frac{1}{2}$ tablespoons cornstarch and 1 cup water in a saucepan and mix over low heat until incorporated. Add this to the lobster or crawfish and stir through. Season with salt, to taste, set aside for 5 minutes, and serve. Serves 4.

suquet de peix . . . . serves 4 to 6

THIS DISH IS ONE OF THE MYRIAD OF FISH AND SEAFOOD STEWS—ALMOST SOUPS—THAT CAN BE FOUND IN SPAIN'S CATALAN-SPEAKING REGION, WHICH INCLUDES THE BALEARIC ISLANDS AND VALENCIA. *SUQUET*, FROM THE VERB *SUQUEJAR*, MEANING "TO SEEP," IMPLIES THAT THE FLAVORS OF THE FISH SEEP INTO THE SAUCE.

olive oil	4 teaspoons
carrot	1, finely diced
onion	1, finely diced
leek	1, finely diced
garlic	3 cloves, chopped
small red chili	1, seeded and finely chopped
celery	1 stalk, finely diced
potatoes	2 large, cut into 3/4-inch dice
firm white fish fillets	1 lb. 2 oz., cut into 3/4-inch dice, reserving any bones and scraps
bay leaf	1
white wine	1 cup
brandy	2 tablespoons
diced tomatoes	14-oz. can, drained
tomato paste	1/4 cup
mussels	12, debearded and scrubbed
raw jumbo shrimp	8, peeled and tails removed
lemon juice	3 tablespoons
Italian parsley	3 tablespoons chopped

Heat the oil in a large saucepan over medium heat. Add the carrot, onion, leek, garlic, chili, and celery and cook for 5 minutes or until the onion is translucent. Add the potatoes and 6 cups cold water. Bring to a boil, then reduce the heat and simmer for 8 minutes or until the potatoes are semicooked. Stir in the fish bones, scraps, and bay leaf and simmer for 6–8 minutes or until the potatoes are soft. Strain the liquid and reserve. Remove the bones, scraps, and bay leaf, and purée the remaining potato and vegetable mixture with the reserved liquid.

In a separate saucepan, combine the wine, brandy, diced tomatoes, and tomato paste and bring to a boil. Add the mussels and cook, covered, for 3 minutes or until opened. Remove from the pan, discarding any mussels that remain closed.

Stir the mussel liquid into the potato purée. Transfer to a large saucepan and bring to a boil. Add the fish pieces and shrimp, reduce the heat, and simmer for 8 minutes or until all the seafood is cooked.

Stir in the mussels and lemon juice and gently heat through. Season well and garnish with the parsley. This dish is delicious served with fried bread and allioli (page 48).

Prepare the mussels by scrubbing them, then removing the beard.

Cook the mussels in the tomato mixture until they open.

zarzuela de pescado

serves 6 to 8

THIS CATALAN FISH SOUP IS NAMED AFTER A STYLE OF LIGHT OPERA, WHICH GIVES SOME IDEA OF ITS VITALITY. IT INCORPORATES A VARIETY OF SEAFOOD AND IS BUILT AROUND A *PICADA*, DESCRIBED AS THE "CATALAN ROUX." A BLEND OF GARLIC, NUTS, AND BREAD, A *PICADA* IS USED TO GIVE FORM TO, OR HOLD TOGETHER, DISHES.

red mullet fillets	10½ oz.
firm white fish fillets	14 oz.
calamari	10½ oz., cleaned
fish stock	6 cups
olive oil	⅓ cup
onion	1, chopped
garlic	6 cloves, chopped
small red chili	1, chopped
sweet *pimentón* (paprika)	1 teaspoon
saffron threads	a pinch
white wine	⅔ cup
crushed tomatoes	14-oz. can
raw medium shrimp	16, peeled and deveined, tails intact
brandy	3 tablespoons
black mussels	24, debearded and scrubbed
Italian parsley	4 teaspoons chopped, to garnish

picada

olive oil	3 tablespoons
day-old bread	2 slices, diced
garlic	2 cloves
blanched almonds	5, roasted
Italian parsley	3 tablespoons

Cut the fish and calamari into 1½-inch pieces. Pour the stock into a large saucepan, bring to a boil, and heat for about 20 minutes or until reduced by half.

To make the *picada*, heat the olive oil in a frying pan, add the bread, and stir for 3 minutes or until golden, adding the garlic for the last minute. Process the bread, garlic, almonds, and parsley in a food processor. Add enough stock to make a smooth paste.

Heat 3 tablespoons of the oil in a large saucepan, add the onion, garlic, chili, and *pimentón,* and cook, stirring, for 1 minute. Add the saffron, white wine, tomatoes, and stock. Bring to a boil, then reduce the heat and leave to simmer.

Heat the remaining oil in another frying pan over medium heat and cook the fish and calamari for 3–5 minutes. Remove from the pan. Add the shrimp, cook for 1 minute, and then add the brandy. Carefully ignite the brandy and let the flames burn down. Remove the shrimp from the pan.

Add the mussels to the hot stock and simmer, covered, for about 3 minutes or until opened. Discard any that do not open. Return all the seafood to the saucepan, add the *picada*, and stir until the sauce has thickened slightly and the seafood is cooked. Season to taste. Serve garnished with parsley.

Cut the fish into cubes, then cut the calamari in the same way.

Process the *picada* ingredients to a paste, adding stock to thin it.

rice

There is a story from Valencia, the traditional home of paella, that dates from the War of Independence fought against France (1808–1814). So impressed was a French general with the paella cooked by a local woman that he promised that for each new rice dish she cooked, he would free a Spanish prisoner of war. He was removed from his post after she had cooked 176 dishes—and she hadn't finished yet.

This anecdote is a polite Spanish way of saying there is more to Spanish rice dishes than paella, which, you might be surprised to know, in its original incarnation as *paella valenciana de la huerta* (Valencian paella from the vegetable garden) does not contain fish or shellfish.

Paella originated in the fertile coastal strip of the Ebro River delta region near Valencia. Its ingredients included rabbit, chicken, tomato, saffron, local dried beans, and green beans, and always, after that, controversy. Rosemary? No! Yes! Peas? Yes! No! There will always be debate in Valencia about the true ingredients of a paella.

Today, of course, we make paella with seafood. And why not? A cuisine that doesn't adapt and change ends up in a museum. But we should not forget the other remarkable rice dishes of Spain, including the classic Valencian dish *arroz con judias blancas y nabos* (rice with white beans and turnips), which many claim is the greatest rice dish of all; or *arroz negro* (rice blackened with squid ink), also from Valencia; or *arroz al horno* (baked rice with chickpeas and garlic) from the Balearic Islands.

To make this multitude of rice dishes, there is a range of short-grained rice varieties, two of the most famous being Calasparra from the Murcian Segura River valley, which has a Denominación de Origen (DO), and the highly absorbent and nutty-flavored Bomba from Valencia, a variety originally planted by the Moors.

seafood paella ....serves 4

PAELLA IS THE DISH BY WHICH SPANISH FOOD IS DEFINED INTERNATIONALLY. IT ORIGINATED IN THE RICE-GROWING EBRO RIVER DELTA AREA, INLAND FROM THE CITY OF VALENCIA, BUT NOW FIRMLY BELONGS, WITH DELICIOUS SEAFOOD ADDED, TO THE WHOLE COUNTRY.

white wine	1/2 cup
red onions	1 1/2, finely chopped
black mussels	12–16, debearded and scrubbed
olive oil	1/2 cup
bacon	1 slice, finely chopped
garlic	4 cloves, crushed
red bell pepper	1, seeded and finely chopped
vine-ripened tomato	1, peeled and chopped
chorizo	3 1/2 oz., thinly sliced
cayenne pepper	a pinch
paella or short-grain rice	1 cup
saffron threads	1/4 teaspoon
chicken stock	2 cups, heated
fresh or frozen peas	1/2 cup
raw shrimp	12, peeled and deveined, tails left intact
squid tubes	2, cleaned and cut into rings
white fish fillets	4 oz., skinned and cut into pieces
Italian parsley	3 tablespoons finely chopped

Heat the wine and two-thirds of the onions in a saucepan. Add the mussels, cover, and gently shake the pan for 5 minutes over high heat. Remove from the heat, discard any mussels that did not open, and drain, reserving the liquid. Heat the oil in a large heavy-based frying pan, add the remaining onions, bacon, garlic, and bell pepper, and cook for 5 minutes. Add the tomato, chorizo, and cayenne pepper. Season. Stir in the reserved liquid, then add the rice and stir again.

Blend the saffron with the stock, then stir into the rice mixture. Bring to a boil, then reduce the heat to low and gently simmer, uncovered, for 15 minutes without stirring.

Put the peas, shrimp, squid, and fish on top of the rice. Push them in, cover, and cook over low heat for 10 minutes, turning the seafood over halfway through cooking time, until the rice is tender and the seafood is cooked through. Add the mussels for the last 5 minutes to heat through. If the rice is not quite cooked, add extra stock and cook for a few more minutes. Remove from the heat for 5 minutes, then sprinkle the parsley over and serve.

Prepare all the seafood first; peel and devein the shrimp.

Add the rice to the paella, stirring to incorporate it.

txangurro . . . . serves 4

THE BASQUE WORD FOR CRAB IS THE NAME GIVEN TO THIS JUSTLY CELEBRATED DISH OF CRAB STUFFED WITH ITS OWN MEAT, WINE, AND GARLIC. IT IS A DELICIOUS ILLUSTRATION OF THE BASQUE GENIUS FOR DEVISING SEAFOOD DISHES THAT COMPLEMENT THE FLAVOR OF THE CENTRAL INGREDIENT—IN THIS CASE, THE CRAB.

live large-bodied crabs, such as centollo or spider	4, weighing about 1 lb. 10 oz. each
olive oil	1/3 cup
onion	1, finely chopped
garlic	1 clove
dry white wine	1/2 cup
puréed tomato	1 cup
dry breadcrumbs	3 tablespoons
Italian parsley	3 tablespoons chopped
butter	3 tablespoons, chopped into small pieces

Put the crabs in the freezer for 45 minutes, so they will lose consciousness. Bring a large sauce pan of water to a boil. Stir in 1/4 cup salt, then add the crabs. Return to a boil and simmer, uncovered, for 15 minutes. Remove the crabs from the water and allow to cool for 30 minutes. Extract the meat from the legs. Open the body without destroying the upper shell, which is needed for serving, reserving any liquid in a bowl. Take out the meat and add to the leg meat. Finely chop all the meat. Scoop out all the brown paste from the shells and mix with the chopped meat.

Heat the olive oil in a frying pan and cook the onion and garlic for 5–6 minutes or until softened. Add the wine and puréed tomato and stir through. Simmer for 3–4 minutes, then add any reserved crab liquid. Simmer for another 3–4 minutes. Add the crab meat and season with salt and freshly ground black pepper. Simmer for 5 minutes or until thick. Discard the garlic.

Preheat the oven to 415°F. Rinse out and dry the crab shells. Spoon the crab mixture into the shells, leveling the surface. Combine the breadcrumbs and parsley, and sprinkle over the top. Dot with butter and bake for 6–8 minutes or until the butter melts and the breadcrumbs brown. Serve hot.

Pick out the cooked crab meat from the legs and body.

Sprinkle the breadcrumbs and parsley over the shells and bake.

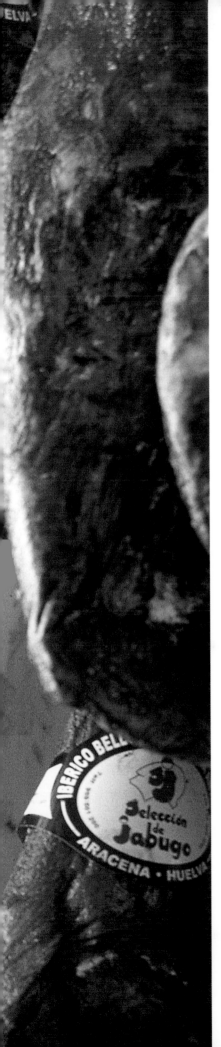

Let's admit it. While Spain's modern cooking, *la nueva cocina*, is lauded by many as the world's most exciting cuisine today, most of us are more than happy with the simple and satisfying home cooking that is found throughout Spain. If you turn your back on the teeming cities and tourist towns along the coast and head for the hills, you will discover a surprising truth. No country in Europe has so much wilderness, so many rugged mountain ranges. In Asturias, for example, the Picos de Europa, Europe's largest national park, is a mountain range comprising three towering massifs, divided by gorges only 9.3 miles from the coast. Meandering through the Picos are cold, clear rivers filled with trout and salmon, when in season, and villages still so remote as to be cut off from car access. This region is so wild that wolves are a continuing problem for livestock farmers.

Half an hour from Madrid begins the Sierra de Guadarrama, behind Gerona lie the mountains of the Cantabrian Range, and south of Granada is the Sierra Nevada, with the highest mountains in Europe, reaching nearly 11,480 feet. Driving along these precipitous mountain roads, you see a sign on many farm gates: *coto de caza* (hunting reserve). In these private reserves, men hunt partridges, pheasants, woodcocks, hares, and wild boars—and not just for the sport, but also for the table. The Spanish repertoire is heavy with recipes for game, such as *morteruelo* (partridge and hare stew) and *codornices con aceitunas* (quail with olives).

Not just animals are hunted in those mountain passes. The damp forests of Galicia, Navarra, and the Basque country are alive with various wild mushrooms in season. You'll find an abundance of morels, chanterelles, and porcinis, all with local names.

Mountain dishes are different in more ways than just the types of ingredients. Clambering up and down all day creates gargantuan appetites and dishes to satisfy them. Your first proper *fabada asturiana* (a stew of the local *faba* beans, chorizo, *morcilla*, pig's ear, and hocks, eaten in the Picos) will leave you stunned and very full. There is also the lip-smacking, rib-tickling *cocido madrileño*, not so much a dish as an entire meal, consisting of a soup and meat course, served separately—both with a glass of ink-black *tempranillo* from the Ribero del Duero. And, if you really love your beef, seek out the restaurants near the bull rings that specialize in cuts of fighting bulls. Once there, you must try the famous stew *rabo de toro*. And yes, you can eat the testicles, deep-fried.

gazpacho .... serves 4

THE ANDALUSIANS HAVE DEVISED MANY WAYS TO DEAL WITH THE SEARING HEAT OF THEIR SUMMERS, AND ONE OF THE BEST IS THE COLD SOUP. GAZPACHO, THE MOST FAMOUS OF THESE WONDERFULLY REFRESHING SOUPS, IS SIMPLICITY ITSELF TO MAKE — AND EVEN EASIER TO EAT.

vine-ripened tomatoes	8 medium
day-old white crusty bread	2 slices, crusts removed, broken into pieces
red bell pepper	1, seeded and roughly chopped
garlic	2 cloves, chopped
small green chili	1, chopped, optional
sugar	1 teaspoon
red wine vinegar	3 tablespoons
extra-virgin olive oil	3 tablespoons

garnish

cucumber	1/2, seeded and finely diced
red bell pepper	1/2, seeded and finely diced
green bell pepper	1/2, seeded and finely diced
red onion	1/2, finely diced
vine-ripened tomato	1/2, diced

Score a cross in the base of each tomato. Put in a bowl of boiling water for 10 seconds, then plunge into cold water and peel away the skin from the cross. Cut the tomatoes in half and scoop out the seeds with a teaspoon. Chop the tomato flesh.

Soak the bread in cold water for 5 minutes, then squeeze out any excess liquid. Put the bread in a food processor with the tomatoes, bell pepper, garlic, chili, sugar, and red wine vinegar and process until combined and smooth.

With the motor running, add the oil to make a smooth, creamy mixture. Season to taste. Refrigerate for at least 2 hours. Add a little extra vinegar, if desired.

To make the garnish, mix together the ingredients. Spoon the chilled gazpacho into soup bowls, top with a little of the garnish, and serve the remaining garnish in separate bowls on the side to add as desired.

Soak the bread briefly in water, then squeeze out excess liquid.

Prepare the cucumber for the garnish by seeding it, then dicing.

ajo blanco . . . . serves 4 to 6

YOUR FIRST ENCOUNTER WITH THIS COOL, SILKY-SMOOTH SOUP WITH PALE GREEN GRAPES AND CROUTONS FLOATING ON TOP WILL ASTONISH AND DELIGHT YOU. IT IS ANOTHER SURVIVOR FROM THE MEDIEVAL MOORISH CUISINE OF THE MEDITERRANEAN, WITH ITS CHARACTERISTIC USE OF GROUND ALMONDS TO THICKEN IT.

day-old white crusty bread	6 slices, crusts removed
whole blanched almonds	1 cup
garlic	3–4 cloves, chopped
extra-virgin olive oil	1/2 cup, plus 3 tablespoons, extra
sherry or white wine vinegar	1/3 cup
vegetable stock	1 1/4–1 1/2 cups
sea salt	to season
day-old white crusty bread	2 1/2 slices, extra, crusts removed and cut into 1/2-inch cubes
seedless green grapes	1 1/4 cups small

Soak the 7 oz. bread in cold water for 5 minutes, then squeeze out any excess liquid. Put the almonds and garlic in a food processor and process until ground. Add the bread and process until smooth.

With the motor running, add the oil in a steady slow stream until the mixture is the consistency of thick mayonnaise (add a little water if the mixture is too thick). Slowly add the sherry or vinegar and 1 1/4 cups of the stock. Blend for 1 minute. Season with sea salt. Refrigerate for at least 2 hours. The soup will thicken so you may need to add stock or water to thin it.

When ready to serve, heat the extra oil in a frying pan, add the extra bread cubes, and toss over medium heat for 2–3 minutes or until golden. Drain on paper towels. Serve the soup very cold. Garnish with the grapes and bread cubes.

Although usually called *ajo blanco de Malaga*, this soup is just as common in the city of Córdoba, once the capital of al-Andalus, and the center of Moorish culture. There are some pitfalls to avoid when making these cold Andalusian soups. First, never add ice cubes. The extra-virgin olive oil and vegetable juices form an emulsion with the cold water, which provides texture, and the melting ice cubes would interfere with that texture, leaving suspicious pools of water on the soup. When making gazpacho, use only ripe, red tomatoes, not tomato paste. And neither gazpacho nor *ajo blanco* needs any spices other than sea salt.

jamón

There is often confusion over what is the difference between *jamón* and prosciutto. Most important, true *jamón* is made from the flesh of the Iberian pig, the famous *pata negra* ("black foot," so named for its black coat), an animal whose recent revival has ensured the continuity of the magnificent *jamónes* of Spain.

The Iberian pig's natural habitat is the *dehesa*, the sparse Mediterranean woodlands populated by oak and holm oak trees. Iberian hams include Denominación de Origen (DO) products from Jabugo, Teruel, Dehesa de Extremadura, Guijuelo, and Huelva.

Serrano is the name given to any ham made not from the flesh of the *pata negra* but from white-coated pigs. The best of these hams are *serrano consorcio* and *serrano especial*, and those from the town of Trevélez in the Alpujarras.

The second difference between *jamón* and prosciutto is the curing. Prosciutto is rubbed with salt, while *jamón* is packed in salt for several months, then hung and air-cured in the dry mountain air for up to three years. A slice of three-year-old Jabugo Gran Reserva with a glass of old amontillado sherry is one of life's great food experiences.

Of course not all pork is turned into ham. Much of it is used in making *embutidos*—sausages of various sorts, cured and fresh. There are countless regional cooked and dried meats, the best known and best traveled being chorizo, made of chopped or ground pork and either sweet or hot *pimentón* (paprika), garlic, and black pepper. It is sold dried for slicing and using as you would salami or fresh for cooking in various dishes, most commonly with beans.

In Catalonia you will find *botifarra negra*, a sausage made of pig's blood, pork fat, some lean meat, and mild seasonings, and *botifarra blanca*, a coarse white pork sausage seasoned with pepper. *Morcilla*, a blood pudding from Asturias, is made using pig's blood mixed with either rice or onion and often fennel, anise, and pine nuts. It is an essential ingredient in *fabada*, the Asturian meat and bean stew.

Everywhere you will find *salchicha* (fresh pork sausage in links) and *salsichón*, a hard, cured sausage called *longaniza* (or *fuet* if long and thin).

caldo gallego

SIMPLY MEANING "GALICIAN BROTH," THIS DISH IS SERVED AND COOKED IN ALL GALICIAN RESTAURANTS AND IN MOST GALICIAN HOMES DURING WINTER. IT CAN ACCOMMODATE AS MANY DIFFERENT INGREDIENTS AS THERE ARE COOKS MAKING IT. THIS VERSION WOULD BE INSTANTLY RECOGNIZED — AND ENJOYED — IN ITS HOME REGION.

dried white kidney beans, such as navy beans	1 1/4 cups
smoked ham hock	1 lb. 2 oz.
olive oil	3 tablespoons
leek	1, washed and chopped
garlic	1 clove, chopped
pork baby back or American-style ribs	1 lb. 2 oz., separated into 2-inch widths
potatoes	2 medium, peeled and cubed
bay leaf	1
Swiss chard	10 stalks, washed well and chopped

Rinse the beans, then soak them in cold water for at least 5 hours. Put the ham hock in a large, heavy-based saucepan and cover with cold water. Bring to a boil, then reduce the heat and simmer for about 1 hour or until the meat starts to come away from the bone and is tender. Allow the hock to cool. When cool enough to handle, remove the meat from the bone and cut into 3/4-inch cubes. Reserve 2 1/2 cups of the cooking liquid.

Meanwhile, put the beans in a large saucepan and cover with cold water. Bring to a boil, then reduce the heat and simmer for 30 minutes or until tender. Drain the beans, reserving 1 cup of the cooking liquid.

Heat the olive oil in a large, heavy-based saucepan over medium heat and cook the leek and garlic for about 5 minutes or until translucent. Add the ham, beans, ribs, potatoes, bay leaf, and reserved cups of cooking liquid (make sure the food is covered with liquid).

Bring to a boil, then reduce the heat, cover, and simmer for 45 minutes. Stir in the Swiss chard and cook for an additional 5 minutes. Season before serving.

Prepare the beans by rinsing, then soaking them in cold water.

Remove the cooked meat from the bone and cut into cubes.

cocido madrileño .... serves 6 to 8

A COCIDO CAN—AND USUALLY DOES—CONTAIN ANY TYPE OF MEAT AT HAND, PLUS CHICKPEAS. THE ONE NECESSARY CONSTANT, ACCORDING TO THE OLD SONG, "COCIDITO MADRILEÑO" ("LITTLE STEW FROM MADRID"), IS "ALL THE CHARM AND THE SPICE/THAT A WOMAN'S LOVE PUTS RIGHT/INTO THE *COCIDITO MADRILEÑO*."

dried chickpeas	1 cup
chicken	2 lb. 4 oz., trussed
beef brisket	1 lb. 2 oz., in one piece
smoke-cured bacon	9-oz. piece
tocino, bacon, or speck	4½ oz.
pig's foot	1
chorizo	7 oz.
onion	1, studded with 2 cloves
bay leaf	1
morcilla blood sausage	1, optional
green beans	3 cups, trimmed and sliced lengthwise
cabbage	⅛ head, cut into sections through the heart
Swiss chard	3 stalks, washed well
potatoes	4 small
leeks	2, cut into 4 inch lengths
saffron threads	a pinch
dried rice vermicelli	2¾ oz.

Soak the chickpeas in cold water overnight. Drain and rinse. Tie loosely in a muslin bag.

Put 12 cups cold water in a very large, deep saucepan. Add the chicken, beef, bacon, and tocino, and bring to a boil. Add the chickpeas, pig's foot, and chorizo, return to a boil, and then add the onion, bay leaf, and ½ teaspoon salt. Simmer, partially covered, for 2½ hours (skim the surface if necessary).

After 2 hours, bring a saucepan of water to a boil, add the *morcilla*, if using, and gently boil for 5 minutes. Drain and set aside. Tie the green beans loosely in a muslin bag. Pour 4 cups water into the saucepan and bring to a boil. Add the cabbage, Swiss chard, potatoes, leeks, and saffron with 1 teaspoon salt. Return to a boil and simmer for 30 minutes. Add the green beans in the last 10 minutes of cooking.

Strain the stock from both the meat and vegetable pans and combine in a large saucepan. Bring to a boil, adjust the seasoning, and stir in the vermicelli. Simmer for 6–7 minutes. Release the chickpeas and pile them in the center of a large, warm platter. Discard the tocino, then slice the meats and sausages. Arrange in groups around the chickpeas at one end of the platter. Release the beans. Arrange the vegetables in groups around the other end. Spoon a little of the simmering broth (minus the vermicelli) over the meat, then pour the rest into a soup tureen, along with the vermicelli. Serve at once. It is traditional to serve both dishes together, although the broth is eaten first.

three ways with legumes

OF ALL THE LEGUMES USED IN SPANISH COOKING, THE CHICKPEA (GARBANZO) IS THE MOST IMPORTANT. EASILY GROWN ON ARID LAND, IT PROVIDES AFFORDABLE FLAVOR AND NOURISHMENT AND IS HIGHLY VERSATILE. ANOTHER IMPORTANT LEGUME, ONE DIFFICULT TO FIND OUTSIDE SPAIN, IS THE ASTURIAN *FABA*, USED IN THE *FABADA ASTURIANA*. IF YOU CAN'T FIND *FABAS*, USE ANY WHITE BEAN (IN SPANISH, *ALUBIA*). *LENTEJAS* (LENTILS), HERE TEAMED WITH CHORIZO, ARE WIDELY USED ALL OVER THE MEDITERRANEAN.

stewed lentils with chorizo

Rinse 2 cups green lentils, then cover with cold water and soak for 2 hours. Heat 4 teaspoons olive oil in a large saucepan over medium heat and add 2 crushed garlic cloves, 1 seeded and diced green bell pepper, and 1 chopped onion. Cook for 5 minutes or until translucent. Add the drained lentils, 2 teaspoons sweet *pimentón* (paprika), 1 bay leaf, and about 1/4 cup olive oil. Cover with water, bring to a boil, and then reduce the heat and gently simmer for 30 minutes or until tender. Meanwhile, heat 4 teaspoons olive oil in a frying pan. Add 2 finely sliced bacon slices, 7 oz. sliced chorizo, and another chopped onion and fry until golden. Add to the lentil mixture with 1 chopped vine-ripened tomato and a large pinch of salt and cook for another 5 minutes. Drizzle a little extra-virgin olive oil over the top and serve. Serves 4.

chickpeas and swiss chard

Soak 1 1/4 cups dried chickpeas in water overnight. Drain and rinse the chickpeas and put in a large saucepan with 1 diced carrot, 1 Italian parsley sprig, 1 bay leaf, and 1 chopped onion. Cover with 3 cups water, bring to a boil, and cook for about 20 minutes or until the chickpeas are almost tender. Add 2 teaspoons salt and 3 tablespoons extra-virgin olive oil and cook for 10 minutes. Heat another 3 tablespoons oil in a frying pan, add 1 chopped garlic clove and another chopped onion, and cook briefly. Add 2 chopped tomatoes and cook for 5 minutes. Stir the tomato mixture and 2 chopped Swiss chard stalks into the chickpea mixture (it should be wet enough to be saucy but not too soupy). Cook for 5 minutes or until the chard is tender. Season well and serve garnished with 2 hard-boiled eggs. Serves 4.

fabada asturiana

Rinse 2 cups dried white kidney beans (such as navy beans) and soak them overnight in cold water. Put 1 lb. 9 oz. smoked ham hock in a large saucepan and cover with water. Bring to a boil, then reduce the heat and simmer for at least 1 hour or until the meat is tender and starting to come away from the bone. Cool, then remove the meat from the bone and cut into 3/4-inch cubes. Reserve 4 cups of the cooking liquid. Heat 3 tablespoons olive oil in a large, heavy-based saucepan and add 5 1/2 oz. chopped bacon, 1 chopped brown onion, and 2 chopped garlic cloves. Cook for 5 minutes or until translucent. Add the beans, cubed ham, a pinch of saffron threads, 1 teaspoon sweet *pimentón* (paprika), and 1 bay leaf, and season with salt and freshly ground black pepper. Add the reserved cooking liquid, bring to a boil, and then reduce the heat and simmer for at least 1 hour or until the beans are cooked (they should be soft but not mushy). Add 7 oz. each of sliced blood sausage (preferably *morcilla*) and chorizo. Cook for 5 minutes or until heated through. Season before serving. Serves 4.

gypsy stew

THE GYPSIES, OR *GITANOS*, HAVE BEEN AN IMPORTANT PART OF SPAIN'S CULTURAL LIFE FOR HUNDREDS OF YEARS. THERE ARE VARIOUS DISHES LIKE THIS ONE (USUALLY MEATLESS), ALL CALLED *OLLA GITANA*. WHY THEY ARE NAMED AFTER THEM IS, LIKE MUCH ABOUT THE GYPSIES, A MYSTERY. NO MATTER, JUST EAT; IT'S DELICIOUS.

dried white kidney beans, such as navy beans	1 1/4 cups
olive oil	1/3 cup
garlic	2 cloves, chopped
onions	2, chopped
sweet *pimentón* (paprika)	1 teaspoon
smoked *pimentón* (paprika)	1 teaspoon
ground cumin	2 teaspoons
ground cinnamon	1/4 teaspoon
cayenne pepper	1/4 teaspoon
dried rosemary	1 teaspoon
red bell pepper	1, seeded and diced
pork tenderloin	1 lb. 10 oz., cut into dice
chopped tomatoes	14-oz. can
chicken stock	1 cup
firm potato or orange sweet potato	2 medium, peeled and cut into large dice
Swiss chard	1 small stalk, washed well and shredded

Cover the beans with cold water and soak for at least 3 hours. Drain well. Preheat the oven to 315°F. Heat 3 tablespoons of the oil in a large saucepan over medium heat, add half the garlic and half the onions, and cook for 5 minutes or until soft. Add the beans and cover with water. Bring to a boil, then reduce the heat and simmer for 45 minutes or until the beans are soft but not mushy.

Meanwhile, heat the remaining oil in a large flameproof casserole dish over medium heat. Add the remaining garlic and onions and cook for 5 minutes or until translucent. Stir through the spices, rosemary, bell pepper, and diced pork and cook until the pork is pale brown all over. Add the tomatoes and stock, bring to a boil, and then cover and cook in the oven for about 1 hour. Add the beans, sweet potato, add 1 cup water, and return to the oven for 30 minutes or until the sweet potato is tender. Stir in the Swiss chard and cook for 5 minutes or until the Swiss chard is wilted. Season to taste before serving.

Beans such as kidney beans are an important part of the Spanish diet, especially in the north of the country. In particular, the country stews are full of beans whose names change as you cross borders or switch towns. For example, the *haba*, or the fava bean, is used throughout Spain, while more or less the same bean, only grown locally, is the Asturian *faba*. This is the king of beans, the star of the famed *fabada Asturiana*, and the market for *fabas* is conducted like a truffle market, with expert buyers and wily sellers eyeing each other and trying to top one another. When choosing beans for Spanish dishes, choose ones that will stay firm throughout lengthy cooking.

caldereta del condado ....serves 4

THIS LAMB STEW IS FROM THE HUELVA DEHESA, THE SPARSE MEDITERRANEAN WOODLANDS OF THE HUELVA REGION. FOR HUNDREDS OF YEARS THE IBERIAN PIGS AND SHEEP HAVE ROAMED HERE, AND THE ORIGINS OF THIS DISH CAN BE TRACED BACK TO THE TRADITIONAL FOOD OF THE SHEPHERDS OF THE REGION.

olive oil	3 tablespoons
onion	1, cut into large dice
carrot	1, cut into large dice
red bell pepper	1, seeded and cut into large dice
garlic	2 cloves, chopped
lamb leg	2 lb. 4 oz., boned and cut into 3/4-inch cubes
ham bone or trimmings	1
chopped tomatoes	14-oz. can
Italian parsley	3 tablespoons chopped
mint	3 tablespoons chopped
tomato paste	3 tablespoons
bay leaves	2
white wine	1 cup
ground cumin	1 teaspoon
sweet *pimentón* (paprika)	1 teaspoon
dry breadcrumbs	1/4 cup
ground cinnamon	1/2 teaspoon

Preheat the oven to 350°F. Heat the olive oil in a large flameproof casserole dish over medium heat and cook the onion, carrot, bell pepper, and garlic until softened. Add the lamb cubes, ham bone or trimmings, the tomatoes, parsley, mint, tomato paste, bay leaves, white wine, and 3/4 cup water. Bring to a boil, then cover and bake in the oven for 1–1 1/2 hours or until the lamb is meltingly tender.

Meanwhile, combine the cumin, *pimentón*, dry breadcrumbs, cinnamon, and a pinch of freshly ground black pepper.

Remove the lamb from the casserole dish with a slotted spoon or tongs and set aside. Discard the bay leaves and ham bone. Purée the remaining liquid and vegetables, return to the casserole, and then stir in the breadcrumb mixture. Cook, stirring, for about 10 minutes or until the sauce has thickened. Return the lamb to the casserole and gently warm through. Serve with green beans.

When very tender, remove the lamb from the casserole dish.

Add the breadcrumb mixture to the sauce and cook until thick.

cochifrito..serves 4 to 6

WHAT THE SPANISH PEOPLE EAT TODAY IS VERY MUCH WHAT THEY HAVE EATEN FOR HUNDREDS OF YEARS. A BOWL OF FILLING, TASTY *COCHIFRITO*, SERVED ON A WINTER'S NIGHT IN FRONT OF A WARM FIRE WITH BREAD AND A GLASS OF LOCALLY MADE WINE, IS AS APPEALING NOW AS IT EVER WAS.

olive oil	1/3 cup
lamb shoulder	2 lb. 4 oz., diced
onion	1 large, finely chopped
garlic	4 cloves, crushed
sweet *pimentón* (paprika)	2 teaspoons
lemon juice	1/3 cup, plus 4 teaspoons, extra
Italian parsley	3 tablespoons

Heat the oil in a large, heavy-based, deep frying pan over high heat and cook the lamb in two batches for 5 minutes each batch or until well browned. Remove all the lamb from the pan.

Add the onion to the pan and cook for 4–5 minutes or until soft and golden. Stir in the garlic and *pimentón* and cook for 1 minute. Return the lamb to the pan with the 1/3 cup lemon juice and 7 cups water. Gently simmer over low heat, stirring occasionally, for 2 hours or until the liquid has almost evaporated and the oil starts to reappear. Stir in the parsley and the extra lemon juice, season with salt and freshly ground black pepper, and serve.

Cook the lamb cubes over high heat until brown all over.

Add the *pimentón* to the onion and garlic and cook until golden.

tripe with chickpeas

LIKE MANY SOUTHERN EUROPEANS, THE SPANISH LOVE THEIR OFFAL. FOR THOSE NEW TO THE CUTS, THIS CLASSIC STEW IS A GOOD BEGINNING. THE TRIPE TAKES ON THE STRONG AND HEARTY FLAVORS OF THE CHORIZO, *PIMENTÓN*, AND GARLIC, THICKENING THE SAUCE AND BINDING THE WHOLE TO THE NUTTY CHICKPEAS.

dried chickpeas	1³/₄ cups
honeycomb tripe	1 lb. 12 oz., bleached and parboiled
olive oil	²/₃ cup
onions	2, chopped
garlic	6 cloves, crushed
sweet *pimentón* (paprika)	3 tablespoons
chorizo	9 oz., sliced
white wine (Spanish if possible)	1¹/₄ cups
chopped tomatoes	14-oz. can
thyme	3 tablespoons chopped
tomato paste	3 tablespoons
long green chilies	2, chopped
bay leaves	2
cloves	8
nutmeg	a pinch
black peppercorns	20
morcilla blood sausage	7 oz., sliced
Italian parsley	1 large handful, chopped

Soak the chickpeas overnight in cold water. Drain and rinse, then transfer to a saucepan and cover with fresh water. Bring to a boil over high heat and simmer for about 30 minutes or until tender. Drain and rinse in cold water. Preheat the oven to 315°F.

Soak the tripe for 10 minutes in water, then rinse and drain. Cut into 2-inch squares. Heat the oil in a large flameproof casserole dish over medium heat and cook the onions and garlic for about 5 minutes or until translucent. Stir in the tripe, pimentón, chorizo, and white wine. Bring to a boil and add the chopped tomatoes, thyme, tomato paste, chilies, bay leaves, cloves, nutmeg, black peppercorns, and salt to taste. Stir in the blood sausage and bake in the oven, covered, for 1¹/₂–2 hours or until the tripe is tender.

Remove the bay leaves from the casserole, add the chickpeas, and bake, covered, for an additional 10 minutes. Serve garnished with the chopped parsley.

The taste for offal has been sadly lost by many English-speaking peoples. As this dish shows, however, there is good reason to overcome this prejudice and give the variety meats (as they are more correctly called) a chance. In a Spanish kitchen, everything is used: pig ears and feet are to be found in a *fabada*, adding to the richness and thickness of the dish in the same way tripe does; kidneys (*riñones*) are seared quickly, then put back in a pan and deglazed with fino sherry; and in Majorca, the great specialty is *frit*, the heart, liver, and lungs of the Easter lamb with fried onion, chili, and red bell pepper. This dish, once tried, will convert even the most timid.

three ways with chicken

THE SPANISH COUNTRY CHICKEN IS DISAPPEARING, BEING REPLACED BY PLUMP BIRDS RAISED IN FACTORY FARMS. ONCE UPON A TIME, YOU COULD BUY CHICKENS WITH SKINS ORANGE FROM PECKING ON THE FALLEN FRUIT FROM THE ORCHARDS THEY GRAZED IN, AND OTHER CHICKENS ENRICHED WITH THE OLIVES FROM THE OLIVE GROVES. THESE THREE RECIPES WOULD BENEFIT FROM BEING MADE WITH FREE-RANGE, ORGANIC CHICKENS FROM SMALL PRODUCERS.

pollo relleno

Preheat the oven to 400°F. Mix together 3½ oz. chopped ham or bacon, 3½ oz. ground pork, 3 tablespoons chopped Italian parsley, 1 crushed garlic clove, a pinch of nutmeg, ½ finely diced onion, 1 teaspoon finely chopped oregano, and 3 tablespoons lemon juice. Add 1 beaten egg and mix with your hands until thoroughly combined. Season well. Wash and pat dry a 3 lb. 8 oz. chicken inside and out, then fill the cavity with the stuffing. Tie the legs together and put the chicken in a shallow roasting pan, coating it with 3 tablespoons olive oil. Season with salt and freshly ground black pepper and roast for 30 minutes. Reduce the heat to 350°F and roast for an additional 35–40 minutes or until the juices run clear when the chicken is pierced between the thigh and body. Allow to rest for 10–15 minutes before carving. Serve a little of the stuffing with each portion of chicken. Serves 4.

chicken cooked with beer

Combine 1½ cups beer (Spanish or Mexican if possible), 4 teaspoons Dijon mustard, 1 teaspoon sweet *pimentón* (paprika), 1 diced brown onion, 1 crushed garlic clove, and a large pinch of salt. Add 2 lb. 12 oz. chicken pieces, toss until well coated, and marinate overnight in the refrigerator. Preheat the oven to 350°F. Heat 3 tablespoons olive oil in a large flameproof casserole dish over medium heat, add 1 seeded and diced green bell pepper, 1 diced brown onion, and 1 crushed garlic clove, and cook for 10 minutes or until softened. Stir in the chicken, marinade, and 14-oz. can chopped tomatoes and season well. Cover and bake for 45–60 minutes or until the chicken is tender. Serves 4.

chicken with samfaina sauce

Cut a 3 lb. 5 oz. chicken into 8 pieces and season with salt and freshly ground black pepper. Heat ¼ cup olive oil in a large heavy-based saucepan over medium heat, add the chicken in batches, and brown well on all sides. Remove the chicken from the pan and reduce the heat to medium-low. Add 2 chopped large brown onions and cook for about 10 minutes or until translucent. Peel 1 medium eggplant and cut into ¾-inch cubes. Cut 4 medium zucchini into strips. Cut 2 seeded green or red bell peppers into ½-inch strips. Add the eggplant, zucchini, and bell peppers to the pan, along with 3 crushed garlic cloves, and cook for 10 minutes or until the vegetables are softened. Stir in two 14-oz. cans chopped tomatoes, 1 bay leaf, 3 tablespoons roughly chopped herbs (such as thyme, oregano, and Italian parsley), and ½ cup white wine. Return the chicken pieces to the pan. Bring to a boil, then cover and simmer over low heat for about 45 minutes or until the chicken is tender and the eggplant is soft. Season well with salt and pepper before serving. Serves 4.

pato con peras .... serves 4

THIS CATALAN FAVORITE WOULD MOST LIKELY BE MADE USING THE DUCK FARMED IN THE AMPURDAN REGION, THE BARBARY, OR MUSCOVY, DUCK (READILY AVAILABLE FROM MOST GOOD POULTRY SUPPLIERS), WHICH ARE LARGE AND HAVE RICH-TASTING MEAT. FOR BEST RESULTS USE AMONTILLADO SHERRY AND VERY FIRM PEARS.

freshly ground nutmeg	1/4 teaspoon
smoked *pimentón* (paprika)	1/2 teaspoon
ground cloves	a pinch
duck	4 lb. 8 oz., jointed into 8 pieces
olive oil	4 teaspoons
bay leaf	1
scallions	8, peeled
baby carrots	8, trimmed
garlic	2 cloves, peeled and sliced
rich, sweet sherry	1/3 cup
thyme	1 sprig
cinnamon stick	1
chicken stock	4 cups
firm ripe pears	4, halved and cored
whole almonds	1/3 cup, roasted
dark bittersweet chocolate	1/4 cup grated

Preheat the oven to 350°F. In a small bowl, mix together the nutmeg, *pimentón*, cloves, and a little salt and freshly ground black pepper. Lightly dust the duck pieces with the spice mixture. Heat the oil in a large flameproof casserole dish, and when hot, brown the duck in batches. Remove from the dish.

Leaving a tablespoon of fat in the casserole, drain off the excess. Add the bay leaf, scallions, and carrots. Cook over medium heat for 3–4 minutes or until lightly browned. Stir in the garlic and cook for an additional 2 minutes. Add the sherry and boil for 1 minute to deglaze the casserole. Stir in the thyme, cinnamon stick, and stock and return the duck to the casserole.

Bring to a boil, then transfer the casserole to the oven and bake, covered, for 1 hour 10 minutes, turning the duck pieces halfway through cooking time. Put the pears on top of the duck and bake for an additional 20 minutes.

Meanwhile, finely grind the almonds in a food processor, then combine with the chocolate.

When the duck is cooked, lift the duck pieces and the pears out of the liquid with a slotted spoon and transfer to a serving dish with the carrots, scallions, and cinnamon stick. Keep warm.

Put the casserole on the stovetop and bring the liquid to a boil. Boil for 7–10 minutes or until the liquid has reduced by half. Add 1/4 cup of the hot liquid to the ground almonds and chocolate and stir to combine. Whisk the paste into the rest of the sauce to thicken. Season to taste, pour over the duck, and serve immediately.

pollo al chilindrón .... serves 4

THE NORTHEASTERN REGION OF ARAGÓN IS HOME TO THIS RICH AND SATISFYING TRADITIONAL CHICKEN DISH. YOU MAY, IF YOU WISH, ADD A GLASS OF A RED OR WHITE WINE FROM THE REGION A FEW MINUTES BEFORE SERVING — AND DRINK THE REST WITH IT.

vine-ripened tomatoes	6
chicken	3 lb. 5 oz., cut into 8 portions
olive oil	1/4 cup
red onions	2 large, cut into 1/4-inch slices
garlic	2 cloves, crushed
red bell peppers	3, seeded and cut into 1/2-inch strips
jamón or prosciutto	2 1/4 oz., finely chopped
thyme	4 teaspoons chopped
sweet *pimentón* (paprika)	2 teaspoons
pitted black olives	8
pitted green olives	8

Score a cross in the base of each tomato. Put in a bowl of boiling water for 10 seconds, then plunge into cold water and peel away the skin from the cross. Cut each tomato in half and scoop out the seeds with a teaspoon. Finely chop the flesh.

Pat the chicken dry with paper towels and season well with salt and freshly ground black pepper. Heat the oil in a heavy-based frying pan over medium heat and cook the chicken a few pieces at a time, skin side down, for 4–5 minutes or until golden. Turn the chicken over and cook for another 2–3 minutes. Transfer to a plate and keep warm.

Add the onions, garlic, bell peppers, *jamón*, and thyme to the frying pan. Cook, stirring frequently, for about 10 minutes or until the vegetables have softened but not browned.

Add the tomatoes and pimentón, increase the heat, and cook for 10–12 minutes or until the sauce has thickened and reduced. Return the chicken to the pan and coat well with the sauce. Cover the pan and reduce the heat to low. Simmer the chicken for 25–30 minutes or until tender. Add the olives and adjust the seasoning, if necessary, before serving.

quails in vine leaves . . . . serves 4

A WIDE VARIETY OF BIRDS ARE USED IN SPANISH COOKING, FROM WELL-FED FARM CHICKENS TO WILD-CAUGHT PHEASANTS AND EVEN PARTRIDGES, WHICH ARE OFTEN SERVED WITH A RICH CHOCOLATE SAUCE. QUAIL, WITH THEIR DELICATE-TASTING FLESH, ARE TREATED MORE SIMPLY, HERE PREPARED WITH *JAMÓN* AND SHERRY.

quail	8
lemons	2
jamón or prosciutto	8 slices
vine leaves	16, in brine, rinsed in cold water
olive oil	4 teaspoons
veal or chicken stock	1/4 cup
sweet sherry	1/2 cup
butter	3 1/2 tablespoons cold, diced
watercress	1/2 bunch

Preheat the oven to 400°F. Wash the quail and pat dry with paper towels. Cut the lemons into quarters and put a quarter inside each quail cavity. Season and wrap each quail with a slice of *jamón*. Put a quail on top of 2 overlapping vine leaves, fold the leaves around the bird, and secure with kitchen twine. Repeat with the remaining quail and leaves.

Put the wrapped quail on a baking sheet, drizzle with the oil, and bake for 30 minutes. Remove from the oven, pierce a quail between the thigh and body through to the bone, and check that the juices run out clear. (If they are pink, return to the oven and cook for an additional 5 minutes.) Transfer the quail to a separate plate to rest for 10 minutes, removing the twine and vine leaves.

Pour the remaining pan juices into a small saucepan with the stock and sherry. Bring to a boil and gradually whisk in the butter, whisking for 3 minutes or until the sauce is slightly shiny. Serve the quail on a bed of watercress, drizzled with the sauce.

Put a lemon wedge in the cavity, then wrap the quail with *jamón*.

Use two vine leaves to wrap each quail, overlapping to cover.

Secure the quail and its wrapping with kitchen twine.

three ways with wine

SPANISH WINE IS FINALLY REVEALING ITSELF TO THE REST OF THE WORLD. THE BLEND OF TECHNOLOGY AND TRADITION, AS WELL AS THE WIDE VARIETY OF SOILS, SITES, AND MICROCLIMATES, PRODUCES WINES OF EXCEPTIONAL QUALITY. WINES RANGE FROM THE TIMELESS SHERRIES AND THOSE MADE USING INDIGENOUS SPANISH GRAPE VARIETIES (SUCH AS *TEMPRANILLO* AND *ALBARIÑO*) TO POWERFUL MODERN WINES MADE USING FRENCH GRAPES LIKE CHARDONNAY. THE RESULT: AN EMBARRASSMENT OF CHOICES FOR THE SPANISH COOK.

roast leg of lamb

Preheat the oven to 400ºF. Rinse 3 lb. 5 oz. leg of lamb and pat dry with paper towels. Put the lamb in a roasting pan and drizzle 3 tablespoons olive oil and 1 cup white wine (ideally Spanish) over the top. Mix together 1 bunch chopped Italian parsley, 2 teaspoons finely chopped rosemary, 2 teaspoons finely chopped thyme, and 8 crushed garlic cloves. Sprinkle over the lamb, pressing down firmly. Put the lamb in the oven and cook for 20 minutes, basting with the pan juices. Reduce the temperature to 350ºF and cook for 1 hour. Remove from the oven and allow to stand for at least 10 minutes before serving. The lamb will be medium-rare to medium. If you prefer your lamb rare, allow 20–25 minutes cooking time per 1 lb. 2 oz., and for well-done, 30–35 minutes per 1 lb. 2 oz. Serves 4.

oxtail stew

Preheat the oven to 300ºF. Cut 4 lb. 8 oz. oxtails into ³⁄₄-inch-thick pieces. Coat the oxtails with seasoned flour. Heat 3 tablespoons olive oil in a large, heavy-based, flameproof casserole dish over medium heat, add the oxtails in batches, and brown all over. Remove to a plate. Heat another 3 tablespoons olive oil in the casserole over medium heat, add 2 chopped brown onions, 1 diced leek, 2 diced carrots, 1 chopped celery stalk, and 2 crushed garlic cloves, and cook for about 5 minutes or until the vegetables are softened. Stir in 14-oz. can crushed tomatoes, 1¹⁄₂ cups white wine, 1¹⁄₂ cups beef stock, 1 teaspoon sweet *pimentón* (paprika), 1 bay leaf, and 3 tablespoons chopped thyme, and bring to a boil. Add the oxtails, making sure they are covered with liquid (add extra water if necessary), then cover and bake in the oven for 4–5 hours, depending on the size of the oxtails. The meat should easily fall away from the bone when ready. Serve garnished with 3 tablespoons chopped Italian parsley. Serves 4–6.

rabbit in red wine

Joint 2 x 2 lb. 4 oz. rabbits and cut each rabbit into 8 pieces. Season the meat. Heat ¹⁄₄ cup olive oil in a heavy flameproof casserole dish over medium heat. Add the rabbit in batches and cook for about 4 minutes per batch or until golden brown. Remove and set aside. Heat another 2 tablespoons oil in the casserole and cook 1 chopped large brown onion for 5 minutes or until translucent. Add 6 peeled and chopped plum tomatoes and simmer gently for 10 minutes. Stir in 1 teaspoon sweet *pimentón* (paprika), 6 crushed garlic cloves, 3 slices *jamón* or prosciutto, cut into strips, 3¹⁄₂ oz. chopped chorizo, 3 seeded and diced red bell peppers, 3 tablespoons chopped thyme, 1 cup red wine (preferably Spanish), the rabbit pieces, and 3 tablespoons roughly chopped Italian parsley. Check the seasoning. Bring to a boil, then reduce the heat and simmer for 35 minutes or until the rabbit is tender. Remove the rabbit pieces and simmer the sauce for 20–30 minutes or until reduced and shiny. Return the rabbit to the casserole and gently heat through. Season to taste, garnish with a little parsley, and serve. Serves 4.

chicken in
saffron stew

THIS IS A MODERN DISH, USING ONE OF SPAIN'S NATIVE INGREDIENTS, *AZAFRAN* (SAFFRON), AND USING A CLASSIC CATALAN THICKENING AND FLAVORING TECHNIQUE, THE *PICADA*. IN THIS RECIPE THE *PICADA* COMBINES PINE NUTS, CINNAMON, SAFFRON, GARLIC, AND PARSLEY.

olive oil	1/4 cup
pine nuts	1/4 cup
bread	1 thick slice, crusts removed and cut into pieces
ground cinnamon	1/2 teaspoon
saffron threads	a pinch
garlic	2 cloves
Italian parsley	3 tablespoons chopped
chicken	3 lb. 5 oz., cut into 8 pieces and seasoned with salt
brown onions	2, finely chopped
white wine	1/2 cup
chicken stock	1 1/2 cups
bay leaf	1
thyme	2 sprigs
lemon juice	3 tablespoons
egg yolks	2

Heat 4 teaspoons of the oil in a large, heavy-based, flameproof casserole dish over medium-high heat. Add the pine nuts and bread and lightly fry for about 3 minutes or until golden. Remove and drain on paper towels. When cooled slightly, put in a mortar or food processor, add the cinnamon, saffron, garlic, and half the parsley, and pound or process to a coarse, crumbly consistency.

Heat the remainder of the oil in the casserole over medium heat and brown the chicken pieces for about 5 minutes. Remove to a plate. Add the onions to the casserole and cook for 5 minutes or until translucent.

Return the chicken pieces to the casserole with the wine, stock, bay leaf, and thyme, and simmer, covered, over medium heat for 1 hour or until the chicken is tender. Remove the chicken and cover to keep warm. Add the pine-nut paste to the casserole and cook for 1 minute. Remove from the heat and whisk in the lemon juice, egg yolks, and remaining parsley. Return the casserole to the stovetop and stir over very low heat until just thickened slightly (do not allow it to boil or the sauce will split). Season to taste, return the chicken to the casserole, and gently warm through before serving.

Make the *picada* by pounding the nuts, bread, and spices together.

Add the lemon juice, egg, and parsley, whisking to incorporate.

chicken with raisins and pine nuts

....serves 4

SOME INGREDIENTS TURN UP IN SPANISH FOOD TIME AND TIME AGAIN, ALL OVER THE COUNTRY. PINE NUTS AND RAISINS ARE TWO SUCH INGREDIENTS, ALWAYS TOGETHER, LIKE CHORIZO AND CHICKPEAS, AND ALWAYS GOOD. IN THIS SIMPLE DISH, THEY ADD RICHNESS AND SWEETNESS TO THE CHICKEN.

chicken	2 lb. 12 oz.
lemon	1/2, cut into 2 wedges
bay leaves	2
olive oil	1/4 cup
onion	1, thinly sliced
garlic	3 cloves, crushed
chopped tomatoes	14-oz. can
white wine	2/3 cup
sun-dried tomato purée or	
tomato paste	3 tablespoons
red or green bell pepper	1, seeded and cut into thin strips
pitted black olives	1/3 cup
raisins	1/4 cup
pine nuts	3 tablespoons, roasted

Preheat the oven to 400°F. Wash and pat dry the chicken, then season with plenty of salt and freshly ground black pepper. Put the lemon wedges and bay leaves inside the cavity, drizzle with 3 tablespoons of the oil, and roast in the oven for 1 hour. Pierce the chicken between the thigh and body through to the bone and check that the juices run out clear; if they are pink, cook for another 15 minutes.

Meanwhile, heat the remaining oil in a large frying pan over medium heat and cook the onion and garlic for 5 minutes or until translucent. Add the tomatoes and cook for 2 minutes. Stir in the wine, tomato purée, bell pepper, olives, and raisins, and simmer for 6–8 minutes or until the mixture reaches a sauce consistency. Cut the chicken into eight portions, tipping the juice from the chicken cavity into the sauce. Spoon the sauce over the chicken pieces and garnish with the pine nuts.

Season the chicken, then fill the cavity with lemon wedges.

Cook the chicken until golden and the juices run out clear.

While the chicken cooks, prepare the tomato sauce.

three ways with vegetable sides

VEGETABLES ARE TREATED WITH RESPECT IN SPAIN. THE COUNTRYSIDE IS RICH WITH WELL-TENDED MARKET GARDENS, AND IN THE VILLAGES, YOU CAN READ THE SEASONS FROM THE PRODUCE ON DISPLAY: IF THERE ARE BELL PEPPERS, IT MUST BE SUMMER; IF ARTICHOKES AND CAULIFLOWER ABOUND, WINTER HAS ARRIVED. ALL THREE DISHES BELOW CAN BE EATEN AS INTRODUCTIONS TO A MAIN MEAL OR AS A MEAL IN THEMSELVES. *ESCALIVADA*, CATALAN CHARBROILED VEGETABLES, CAN BE FOUND IN RESTAURANTS RIGHT ACROSS SPAIN.

judias verdes en salsa de tomate

Cook 3½ cups trimmed green beans in boiling water for 3–5 minutes or until tender. Drain and set aside. Heat 4 teaspoons olive oil in a frying pan, add 1 finely chopped onion, and cook over medium heat for 5 minutes or until soft. Add 2 finely chopped garlic cloves and cook for 1 minute. Add 4 teaspoons sweet *pimentón* (paprika), ¼ teaspoon chili flakes, and 1 crushed bay leaf, cook for 1 minute, and then stir in 14-oz. can of good-quality crushed tomatoes. Simmer over medium heat for about 15 minutes or until reduced and pulpy. Add the reserved beans and 3 tablespoons chopped Italian parsley and cook for 1 minute or until warmed through. Season to taste. Serve warm or at room temperature. Serves 4.

escalivada

Without slicing through the base, cut 1 red onion from top to bottom into six sections, leaving it attached at the base. Put on a barbecue or charbroil pan with 6 small eggplants, about 6½ inches long, 4 red bell peppers, and 4 orange bell peppers. Cook over medium heat for 10 minutes, turning occasionally, until the eggplants and bell pepper skins are blackened and blistered. Put the bell peppers in a plastic bag for 10 minutes to cool. Set aside the onion and eggplants. Dry-fry 4 teaspoons baby capers with a pinch of salt until crisp. Cut the onion into its six sections and discard the charred outer skins. Peel the skins off the eggplants and remove the stalks. Cut from top to bottom into slices. Peel the bell peppers and remove the seeds. Cut into wide slices. Arrange all the vegetables on a large serving platter. Drizzle over ⅓ cup good-quality olive oil and season to taste with salt and freshly ground black pepper. Sprinkle 4 teaspoons chopped Italian parsley, 2 chopped garlic cloves, and the capers over the top. Serve cold as a salad or warm as an accompaniment to barbecued meats. Serves 4.

swiss chard with raisins and pine nuts

Trim 4 Swiss chard or English spinach stalks, then wash the leaves and shred them. Put 3 tablespoons pine nuts in a frying pan and stir over medium heat for 3 minutes or until lightly browned. Remove from the pan and reserve. Heat 4 teaspoons olive oil in the pan, add 1 halved and sliced small red onion, and cook over low heat, stirring occasionally, for 10 minutes or until translucent. Increase the heat to medium, add 1 thinly sliced garlic clove, and cook for 1 minute. Add the Swiss chard, 3 tablespoons raisins, and a pinch of ground cinnamon. Cover and cook for 2 minutes or until the Swiss chard wilts. Stir in the reserved pine nuts, season to taste, and serve. Serves 6.

catalan-style cannelloni

CANALONS, AS THEY ARE KNOWN IN CATALONIA, ARE JUST ONE OF THE MANY TYPES OF PASTA USED IN THE AREA. THIS DISH IS TYPICAL OF BARCELONA AND IS AN ADAPTATION OF THE ORIGINAL BROUGHT BY ITALIAN MIGRANTS WHO CAME TO THE CITY IN THE NINETEENTH CENTURY.

olive oil	3 tablespoons
ground beef or veal	4$\frac{1}{2}$ oz.
ground pork	4$\frac{1}{2}$ oz.
chicken livers	7 oz., chopped
brown onion	1, diced
leek	1, halved lengthwise and chopped
dry sherry	3 tablespoons
thyme	4 teaspoons chopped
crushed tomatoes	14-oz. can
Italian parsley	$\frac{1}{3}$ cup chopped
butter	5 tablespoons
all-purpose flour	$\frac{1}{2}$ cup
milk	4 cups
nutmeg	a pinch
dried cannelloni tubes	25
tomato paste or passata	$\frac{1}{2}$ cup
manchego or Parmesan cheese	1 cup grated

Preheat the oven to 350°F. Heat the olive oil in a large heavy-based frying pan over medium heat. Cook the beef, pork, chicken livers, onion, and leek for 10 minutes or until the meat is well browned, breaking up any lumps with the back of a wooden spoon. Add the sherry, thyme, tomatoes, and half the parsley, and cook for 3 minutes or until most of the liquid has evaporated. Season and allow to cool.

Melt the butter in a large saucepan over medium heat. Add the flour and cook, stirring with a wooden spoon, for 1–2 minutes or until pale yellow. Remove from the heat and add the milk gradually, stirring constantly until blended. Return to the heat and slowly bring the mixture to a boil, whisking for 15 minutes or until thickened. Season with nutmeg, salt, and freshly ground black pepper.

Fill the cannelloni with the meat mixture using a wide-tip piping bag or a spoon. Put the filled cannelloni side by side in a buttered ovenproof dish. Pour the white sauce over the top and dot with the tomato paste. Top with the grated cheese and bake for 40–45 minutes. Garnish with the remaining chopped parsley.

Use a wooden spoon to break up any lumps in the meat mixture.

Allow the mixture to cool, then use to fill the cannelloni tubes.

fideus a la catalana .... serves 4 to 6

THERE ARE NUMEROUS RECIPES FOR THIS SHORT AND THIN NOODLE, A CURIOSITY OF CATALAN CUISINE. UNLIKE MOST ITALIAN PASTAS, *FIDEUS* IS VERY SHORT—HALF THE LENGTH OF YOUR LITTLE FINGER—AND THIN. BELOW IS A CLASSIC COMBINATION OF *FIDEUS* WITH PORK.

olive oil	⅓ cup
pork spare ribs	9 oz., cut into ½-inch-thick slices
brown onion	1, chopped
tomato paste or passata	½ cup
sweet *pimentón* (paprika)	1 teaspoon
fresh spicy pork sausages	3½ oz., thickly sliced
chorizo	3½ oz., cut into pieces
beef or chicken stock	6 cups
fideus or spaghettini	1 lb. 2 oz.
bread	1 slice
nuts, such as hazelnuts, pine nuts, or almonds	⅓ cup
garlic	2 cloves, crushed
Italian parsley	3 tablespoons chopped
ground cinnamon	¼ teaspoon
saffron threads	¼ teaspoon

Heat the oil in a large heavy-based saucepan over medium-high heat and cook the ribs in batches until golden. Add the onion and cook for 5 minutes or until softened. Stir in the tomato paste and *pimentón* and cook for a few minutes more.

Add the spicy sausages, chorizo, and the stock (reserving 3 tablespoons) and bring to a boil. Reduce to a simmer and add the *fideus* or spaghettini (if using spaghettini, break the pasta into 1-inch pieces before using). Cook, covered, for 15 minutes or until the pasta is al dente.

Meanwhile, toast the bread and remove the crusts. In a mortar or food processor, pound or process the nuts with the garlic, parsley, cinnamon, and bread to make a paste. Stir in the saffron. If the mixture is too dry, add 2–3 tablespoons of the reserved stock. Stir the paste into the pan and simmer for 5 minutes or until it has thickened slightly. Season well before serving.

According to food scholar Charles Perry, it was not the Italians or even the Romans who brought *fideus* to Catalonia, but the Moors, who took the idea from the Greeks. *Fideus*, the original Moorish word, means "abundant" or "overflowing." There is a related Italian pasta, *fedelini*, which is somewhat like an angel-hair pasta. The first mention of *fideus* was in 1429, almost two hundred years before the appearance of *fedelini* in Italian recipes. Unlike Italian pasta, *fideus* is often cooked dry with other ingredients (as opposed to being boiled in water first). If you cannot find *fideus*, spaghettini is a good substitute.

sofregit

Sofregit is a flavor base used in countless Catalan recipes. Though simple, it requires care and time to perfect. Of course, it is related to the Italian *soffritto* and the Spanish *sofrito*, but as the Catalans tend to fuss a little more with all their food, so it is with *sofregit*.

The onions are the most important ingredient. Mild, sweet onions are best, but large red ones are fine. And, although the word *sofregit* means lightly fried, that is in reference to the level of the flame, not the length of cooking time: the onions should be gently stewed, in an abundance of olive oil, for as long as you have patience. They should be deep brown and caramelized but definitely not burned. When finished, pour off the excess oil and reserve for other uses. It goes without saying that you should use the reddest, ripest tomatoes you can find (failing that, and in winter, good-quality canned tomatoes can be used).

Cover the bottom of a large frying pan or flameproof casserole dish with ¹/₂–²/₃ cup extra-virgin olive oil. Heat over medium heat for several minutes, then add 3 roughly chopped onions. Stir the onions into the oil, reduce the heat to very low (even using a simmer pad if you have one), and continue cooking until the onions have reached the desired dark, caramelized state. Add a little water if it threatens to burn. Tip out and reserve the excess oil once the onion is done.

Peel, seed, and chop 6 vine-ripened tomatoes—or use 2 x 14-oz. cans tomatoes—and add to the frying pan or casserole. Continue cooking until the liquid has evaporated and the tomatoes have begun to dissolve into the onion. At this point, if necessary for a specific recipe, add herbs. If you need garlic, add after the onion has finished cooking. *Sofregit* can be stored, under a thin layer of oil, in a screw top or sealed container, for up to three weeks in the refrigerator.

tumbet

THE CLASSIC VEGETABLE DISH OF MAJORCA, TUMBET IS EATEN AS A MEAL IN ITS OWN RIGHT, EITHER HOT OR COLD OR AS AN ACCOMPANIMENT TO BAKED *LAMPUGA* (MAHI MAHI OR DOLPHIN FISH) DURING ITS SHORT MEDITERRANEAN AUTUMN SEASON.

olive oil	1 cup
waxy potatoes, such as desiree, fingerling, or Pontiac	3 medium, cut into 1/4-inch rounds
eggplant	1 large, cut into 1/4-inch rounds
green bell peppers	2 medium, seeded and cut into 1 1/4-inch pieces
Italian parsley	1 large handful, roughly chopped

tomato sauce

vine-ripened tomatoes	8 medium
olive oil	3 tablespoons
garlic	3 cloves, crushed
red onion	1, finely chopped
thyme	2 teaspoons chopped

To make the tomato sauce, score a cross in the base of each tomato and put in a bowl of boiling water for 10 seconds. Plunge into cold water and peel the skin away from the cross. Cut each tomato in half and scoop out the seeds with a teaspoon. Finely chop the tomato flesh.

Heat the oil in a heavy-based frying pan and cook the garlic and onion over low heat for 5–6 minutes or until softened. Increase the heat to medium, add the tomatoes and thyme, and cook for 20 minutes or until thickened. Season to taste. Preheat the oven to 350°F.

While the sauce is cooking, heat the oil in a heavy-based frying pan over low heat and cook the potatoes in batches until tender but not brown. Remove with a slotted spoon or tongs and transfer to a casserole dish measuring about 11 x 8 x 2 inches. Season lightly.

Increase the heat to high and cook the eggplant for 3 minutes each side or until golden, adding a little more oil if necessary. Drain the slices on paper towels, then arrange on top of the potatoes. Season lightly.

Cook the bell peppers in the same pan until tender but not browned, adding a little more olive oil if needed. Remove with a slotted spoon, drain on paper towels, and arrange on the eggplant. Season lightly with salt and freshly ground black pepper. Pour the sauce over the top and bake for about 20 minutes. Sprinkle with the parsley and serve warm as an accompaniment to fish or meat, or serve at room temperature with allioli (page 48).

Cook the eggplant slices over high heat until golden.

Drain the bell pepper strips, then layer them over the eggplant.

huevos a la flamenca .... serves 4

THIS DISH IS ORIGINALLY FROM ANDALUSIA, BUT IT IS NOW FOUND ALL AROUND THE SPANISH PENINSULA. IT IS FULL OF THE COLOR, GUTSY FLAVORS, AND EXUBERANCE OF THE GYPSIES WHO INVENTED FLAMENCO. SERVE IT WITH A BIG RED FROM ALICANTE.

vine-ripened tomatoes	1 lb. 2 oz.
olive oil	1/4 cup
potatoes	3 medium, cut into 3/4-inch cubes
red bell pepper	1, seeded and cut into strips
onion	1, chopped
jamón or prosciutto	3 1/2 oz., thickly sliced
thin green asparagus	8 spears, trimmed
fresh or frozen peas	2/3 cup
baby green beans	1 1/2 cups, sliced
tomato paste	3 tablespoons
eggs	4
chorizo	3 1/2 oz., thinly sliced
Italian parsley	3 tablespoons chopped

Score a cross in the base of each tomato. Put in a bowl of boiling water for 10 seconds, then plunge into cold water and peel away the skin from the cross. Roughly chop the tomatoes.

Heat the oil in a large frying pan or saucepan and cook the potatoes over medium heat for 8 minutes or until golden. Remove with a slotted spoon. Reduce the heat and add the bell pepper and onion to the pan. Cut 2 *jamón* slices into pieces similar in size to the bell pepper and add to the pan. Cook for 6 minutes or until the onion is soft.

Preheat the oven to 350°F. Reserve 4 asparagus spears. Add the rest to the pan with the peas, beans, tomatoes, and tomato paste. Add 1/2 cup water and season with salt and freshly ground black pepper. Return the potato cubes to the pan. Cover and cook over low heat for about 10 minutes, stirring occasionally.

Grease a large, oval, ovenproof dish. Transfer the vegetables to the dish, discarding any excess liquid. Using the back of a spoon, make 4 deep, evenly spaced indentations and break an egg into each. Top with the reserved asparagus and the chorizo. Cut the remaining *jamón* into large pieces and distribute over the top. Sprinkle with the parsley. Bake for about 20 minutes or until the egg whites are just set. Serve warm.

Return the potato to the pan and cook until the vegetables are soft.

Add the eggs to the dish, nestling them among the vegetables.

queso

The world is discovering Spanish food—not just the great chefs and dishes, but also the great food products. Even five years ago, many would have been hard-pressed to name more than one Spanish cheese: manchego.

The truth is, Spain produces—officially—one hundred different types of cheese, twelve of which are covered by a Denominación de Origen label. This official number is just the beginning, however. The market at Cangas de Onis in Asturias, for example, could well have thirty different cheeses for sale.

Most of these cheeses are made by hand by cheesemakers who run their own herds of milking animals. Even a famous cheese like Cabrales, from the Picos de Europa mountains in Asturias, is made by makers in much the same way as it probably was in the time of Pelayo (the legendary eighth-century Visigoth and first king of Asturias), with milk from their own herds—often a mixture of cows, goats, and sheep. It is matured in mountain caves, where the creamy paste acquires its pungent flavor from wild yeasts.

In Extremadura, in Spain's southwest, you will find the cheese that three-Michelin-star chef Juan Mari Arzak considers the best in Spain: Torta de la Serena. Made from raw merino milk, it is a ripe, luscious, oozing, sticky, custard-textured center held (only just) in place by a crusty rind. Scoop it out with a spoon.

One of the finest goat's milk cheeses is the *queso de Murcia al vino*, from the province of Murcia on the east coast. During ripening, the rind is washed twice weekly with local wines, either Tecla or Jumilla, turning the rind red and giving the cheese a lovely floral bouquet and a rich winey flavor.

And of course there is always manchego (pictured, right), the best known of Spain's cheeses, made only from sheep's milk in the provinces of Toledo, Cuenca, Albacete, and Ciudad. The best is nutty and sweet with great palate length. From its provincial homes, manchego travels around Spain and the world. Afuega'l Pitu del Aramo, on the other hand, rarely leaves Temia in Asturias. The name of this tart, dense cow's milk cheese means, in the Asturian dialect, "choke the chicken of Aramo," indicating the method for testing the curd. In ancient times, a small amount of the curd was given to an unfortunate chicken, who choked if it was ready. This is possibly the most ancient cheese produced in Spain but, thankfully, the testing methods have changed somewhat.

andrajos

THE NAME OF THIS ANDALUSIAN DISH MEANS "TATTERS AND RAGS" AND PROBABLY REFERS TO THE WAY IN WHICH THE ORIGINAL RECIPES INCLUDED FLOUR AND WATER FOR MAKING LITTLE SQUARE DUMPLINGS (THE RAGS AND TATTERS). THE SAME EFFECT IS CREATED HERE WITH LASAGNA SHEETS. MEAT WAS ALSO OFTEN INCLUDED.

bacalao (salt cod)	1 lb. 2 oz.
olive oil	3 tablespoons
onion	1, chopped
garlic	2 cloves, finely chopped
crushed tomatoes	14-oz. can
sweet *pimentón* (paprika)	1/2 teaspoon
smoked *pimentón* (paprika)	1/2 teaspoon
saffron threads	a pinch
black peppercorns	10
cumin seeds	1 teaspoon
chicken stock	2 cups
dried lasagna sheets	3 1/2 oz., cut in half to form squares approximately 3 1/2 x 3 1/2 inches
Italian parsley	3 tablespoons chopped
lemon juice	4 teaspoons

Soak the *bacalao* in plenty of cold water for about 20 hours, changing the water four or five times to remove excess salt. Drain, then put the *bacalao* in a large saucepan and cover with cold water. Bring to a boil, then reduce the heat and simmer for 30–45 minutes or until the fish is soft and able to be removed from the bone. Drain, allow to cool, and then shred the *bacalao*.

Heat the oil in a large, heavy-based, flameproof casserole dish over medium heat. Cook the onion and garlic for 5 minutes or until translucent. Add the crushed tomatoes and cook for 2 minutes. Stir in the sweet and smoked pimentón and the shredded fish.

In a mortar or food processor, pound or grind the saffron, peppercorns, and cumin seeds to a powder. Add to the casserole with the chicken stock and simmer for 15 minutes or until reduced to a sauce consistency. Meanwhile, cook the lasagna sheets in boiling water until al dente. Stir the lasagna sheets into the casserole and season to taste. Garnish with the parsley, drizzle the lemon juice over the top, and serve.

So much Spanish food is red with spicy, sweet and smoky *pimentón*, known in English by its Hungarian name, paprika. The best *pimentón* comes from La Vera in Extremadura in western Spain, where it is made using traditional methods. When completely ripe, red bell peppers are dried, smoked, and turned daily for between ten and fifteen days over slow-burning holm oak fires. This results in the characteristically intense smoky aroma and flavor of *la vera pimentón*. After smoking, the bell peppers are stone ground a total of seven times, which creates a silky texture. This slow and laborious stone grinding also protects the *pimentón* from its major enemy—bitterness.

pimientos rellenos . . . . serves 4

MANY VEGETABLE DISHES THOUGHT OF BY NON-SPANIARDS AS "SIDES" WILL TURN UP IN SPANISH HOMES AS DISHES IN THEIR OWN RIGHT. THIS IS ESPECIALLY TRUE OF THE VEGETABLES OF NAVARRA, IN THE COUNTRY'S NORTH, WHICH ARE FAMED ACROSS SPAIN. FROM LA RIOJA IN THAT PROVINCE, COMES THIS SIMPLE FAVORITE.

red bell peppers	4
olive oil	¼ cup
onion	1, chopped
garlic	2 cloves, chopped
ground pork or beef	14 oz.
white wine	½ cup
chopped tomatoes	14-oz. can, drained well
long-grain rice	½ cup, cooked
egg	1, lightly beaten
Italian parsley	3 tablespoons finely chopped

Cut the tops off the bell peppers and reserve them to use as lids. Using a small, sharp knife, carefully cut the internal membrane and seeds away from the bell peppers and discard. Preheat the oven to 350°F.

Heat 3 tablespoons of the olive oil in a frying pan over medium-high heat and cook the onion and garlic for 5 minutes or until lightly golden. Add the pork or beef and brown well. Stir in the wine, then reduce the heat to low and simmer for 10 minutes or until the wine has been absorbed.

Add the tomatoes and simmer for an additional 10 minutes, then add the rice. Remove from the heat and stir in the beaten egg and parsley. Season well.

Stuff the bell peppers with the meat mixture, put the lids on top, and stand upright in an ovenproof dish. Drizzle with the remaining olive oil and bake for 45–50 minutes or until the stuffing is cooked through and the bell peppers are tender. Remove from the oven and allow to stand, covered, for about 5 minutes before serving.

Cut the tops off the bell peppers and reserve.

Remove the membrane and seeds without cutting the flesh.

Fill the bell peppers with the mixture, then replace the tops.

pastries and sweets

Behind Spain's pastries and sweet dishes are tales of conquistadors, Aztecs, Moors, and nuns. Chocolate arrived in Spain from Mexico and was embraced immediately; the Moors brought *turrón*, an almond and honey confection, to Europe via Spain, calling it *halvo* (making it a relative of halva); and the convent nuns created such sublime sweets as *tocino de cielo* (bacon from heaven).

All around Spain, you will find wonderful regional pastries—from Santiago de Compostela in Galicia comes *torta de Santiago*; and from Catalonia, *brazos de gitano* (gypsy's arm rolls), a favorite on feast days. But the most celebrated of Spanish sweets is *turrón*, without which no Spaniard could celebrate Easter or Christmas. In the weeks before these religious festivals, stores fill up with boxes of *turrón blando* (soft), the *turrón duro* (hard) *de Alicante*, or the soft, brown confection called *pan de Cadiz*. Although some say that *turrón* dates from pre-Roman times, it's clear to most food historians that it came with the Moors.

Many of the sweets of Catalonia also came with the Moors, such as the *bisbalenc* (a sort of strudel filled with sweet squash paste and topped with pine nuts and sugar) from the coastal Ampurdan region and *panellets* (marzipan balls coated with broiled pine nuts). Very un-Moorish is the most famous dessert of the region, now on menus all over Spain: *crema catalana* (also called flan catalan). Unlike French crème brûlée, it is made with the addition of lemon juice and cinnamon.

But it is the nuns in the convents of Spain, especially in Andalusia, Extremadura, and Castile, who are the keepers of the traditional sweet recipes. For hundreds of years, these recipes, based on the simplest of ingredients—eggs, sugar, flour, lard or oil, sesame seeds, and cinnamon—were closely guarded secrets, as unchanging as the articles of faith. Many convents have their own specialties. For example, in Osuna, the Dominican Santa Catalina convent makes *capiruletas*, a heavy uncooked custard cream made with egg yolks, sugar, ground almonds, and cinnamon. There are various convents where you can buy desserts called *yemas*, based on candied egg yolks, the most famous of which, *yemas de San Leandro*, were—and still are—made by the nuns of San Leandro in Seville.

Finally it should be noted that the Spanish don't tend to cook sweets in their homes, nor do traditional Spanish restaurants serve a great variety of sweets. At the end of a meal, you are more likely to be offered seasonal fruit, cheese, or a product from the local *pastelería*. Those who insist on dessert when dining out will have to make do with the ever-present crema catalana.

crema catalana .... serves 6

THOSE UNFAMILIAR WITH CATALAN CUISINE MAY LOOK AT THIS DISH AND SAY, "BUT THIS IS THE FRENCH DESSERT CALLED CRÈME BRÛLÉE." A CATALAN WILL LOOK AT A CRÈME BRÛLÉE AND SAY, "THEY'VE STOLEN OUR *CREMA CATALANA*."

milk	4 cups
vanilla bean	1, split lengthwise and seeds scraped out
cinnamon stick	1
lemon	1 small, zest cut into strips
orange zest	2 strips, about 1 1/2 x 3/4 inches
egg yolks	8
superfine sugar	1/2 cup
cornstarch	1/3 cup
soft brown sugar	1/4 cup

Put the milk, vanilla seeds and bean, cinnamon stick, lemon zest, and orange zest into a saucepan and bring to a boil. Simmer for about 5 minutes, then strain and set aside.

Whisk the egg yolks with the superfine sugar in a bowl for 5 minutes or until pale and creamy. Add the cornstarch and mix well. Slowly add the warm milk mixture to the egg and whisk continuously. Return to the pan and cook over medium-low heat, stirring constantly, for 5–10 minutes or until the mixture is thick and creamy. Do not boil, as it will curdle. Pour into six 3/4-cup ramekins and refrigerate for 6 hours or overnight.

When ready to serve, sprinkle the top evenly with brown sugar and broil for 3 minutes or until it caramelizes.

Prepare the vanilla bean by scraping out the seeds.

Slowly add the milk to the egg mixture, whisking constantly.

Cook the custard until it is thick, ensuring it does not boil.

flan de naranja . . . . serves 4

THE ADDITION OF ORANGE MAKES THIS A REFRESHINGLY DELICIOUS VARIATION ON THE OLD FAVORITE, *CREMA CATALANA*, OFTEN THE ONLY DESSERT ON A SPANISH RESTAURANT MENU (ALONG WITH FRUIT AND CHEESE).

superfine sugar	1¼ cups
fresh orange juice	¾ cup plus 1 tablespoon, strained
egg yolks	7, at room temperature
egg	1

Preheat the oven to 325°F. Lightly grease four ½-cup ramekins or molds with cooking oil spray and put in a roasting pan.

Put ⅓ cup of the sugar and ¼ cup water in a small saucepan and stir gently over low heat until the sugar dissolves. Increase the heat to a low boil and cook for about 10 minutes or until the mixture is golden and smells like caramel. Divide the toffee among the molds and swirl to cover the bases.

Put the orange juice and remaining sugar in a small saucepan over low heat and stir gently until the sugar dissolves. Increase the heat, bring to a boil, and cook for 2 minutes or until the mixture is slightly syrupy. Allow to cool for 10 minutes.

Put the egg yolks and egg in a bowl and beat with a wooden spoon until combined. Pour the cooled orange juice onto the eggs, stirring until well combined. Pass the mixture through a sieve, then spoon into the molds.

Pour enough boiling water into the roasting pan to come halfway up the outside of the molds. Bake for 15 minutes, then carefully remove the molds from the water and cool to room temperature. Chill completely in the refrigerator (this will take about 2 hours). When ready to serve, dip the molds in hot water for 10 seconds, then invert onto serving plates.

Add the toffee to the molds, swirling to cover the bases.

Heat the orange juice and sugar until turning slightly thick.

chocolate y churros

Of all the foods the Spanish brought back from the New World (potatoes, tomatoes, bell peppers, and chilies) none was more quickly and enthusiastically embraced than chocolate. There was a simple reason for this. The Aztecs of Mexico told the soldiers in the army of Hernán Cortés that chocolate was an aphrodisiac. Montezuma, the Aztec king, employed twenty women solely to prepare his drinking chocolate, often ceremonially served in leopard-skin cups. The Spanish soldiers observed that chocolate harvest time was accompanied by wild orgies.

But the chocolate drunk by the Aztecs was very different from the drink enjoyed at today's *churrerias* (chocolate and churros shops). The Aztecs spiked their drink with spices, ground flowers, and chili, and added achiote, a seed that dyed the drink red.

As you would expect, this dangerous drink was not welcomed by the Spanish clergy. Even when the aphrodisiac rumor was finally put to bed, there were arguments over whether the drinking of chocolate broke the Lenten fast. Curious, then, that some time later, the bitter drink of the Aztecs was transformed by the nuns at a convent in Guajaca into the delicious concoction enjoyed today, simply by adding sugar. Later, it was accepted by and, indeed, embraced by the clergy—so much so that it became the favored breakfast of the Grand Inquisitor, prepared for him by the nuns in his service—an ironic reminder of Montezuma's chocolate maidens.

Walk into a *churreria* on any morning and you will find revelers on their way home and workers starting the day sitting side by side, dunking their churros in chocolate so thick the churros stand up in it. This *espeso* (thick) chocolate is achieved by the addition of cornstarch. And what is a churro? One of the *frutas del sartén*, a fruit of the frying pan. A flour and water batter is forced through a ridged pipe—which gives the churro its distinctive form—and then carefully piped into boiling hot oil, before being cut into edible lengths. This combination of chocolate and churros, with a small glass of aniseed liqueur, is perhaps the most Spanish way to start the day—or end the night.

churros and
hot chocolate

A SPANIARD WOULD BE PUZZLED BY THE INCLUSION OF THESE RECIPES IN A BOOK—THEY HAVE ONLY TO WALK TO THE CORNER CAFÉ TO BE ABLE TO INDULGE IN THIS EXTREMELY RICH LATE-NIGHT OR BREAKFAST SNACK. FOR THOSE OF US WHO ARE NOT SO LUCKY, HERE IT IS.

sugar	1/2 cup
ground cinnamon	1 teaspoon
butter	2 tablespoons
all-purpose flour	1 1/4 cups
orange zest	1/2 teaspoon finely grated
superfine sugar	1/4 teaspoon
eggs	2
vegetable oil	4 cups, for deep-frying

hot chocolate

cornstarch	3 tablespoons
milk	4 cups, plus 3 tablespoons, extra
good-quality dark chocolate	1 1/3 cups chopped
sugar	to taste

Combine the sugar and cinnamon and spread the mixture out on a plate.

Put the butter, flour, orange zest, superfine sugar, 2/3 cup water, and a pinch of salt in a heavy-based saucepan. Stir over low heat until the butter softens and forms a dough with the other ingredients. Continue to cook for 2–3 minutes, stirring constantly, until the dough forms a ball around the spoon and leaves a coating on the base of the pan.

Transfer the dough to a food processor, and with the motor running, add the eggs. Do not overprocess. If the dough is too soft to snip with scissors, return it to the pan and cook, stirring, over low heat until it is firmer. Spoon the dough into a piping bag fitted with a 1/4-inch star nozzle.

Heat the oil in a wide saucepan to 350°F or until a cube of bread dropped into the oil browns in 15 seconds. Pipe 2-inch to 3-inch lengths of batter into the oil, a few at a time. An easy technique is to pipe with one hand and cut the batter off using kitchen scissors in the other hand.

Cook the churros for about 3 minutes or until puffed and golden, turning once or twice. Drain each batch on paper towels. While still hot, toss them in the sugar mixture and serve at once.

To make the hot chocolate, mix the cornstarch and the extra milk to a smooth paste. Put the chocolate and remaining milk in a saucepan and whisk constantly over low heat until just warm. Stir 3 tablespoons of the chocolate milk into the cornstarch paste, then return all the paste to the milk. Whisking constantly, cook the mixture until it just begins to boil. Remove from the heat, add sugar to taste, and whisk for 1 minute. Serve with the churros.

Pipe lengths of batter into the oil, snipping them off with scissors.

Whisk the chocolate mixture over low heat until warm.

higos rellenos .... serves 6

THE SEASON FOR FRESH FIGS IS SHORT AND INTENSE, BUT SO ABUNDANT ARE THE FIGS OF SPAIN THAT THEY CANNOT ALL BE EATEN AND MANY ARE DRIED. INGENIOUS METHODS OF USING THESE DRIED FIGS HAVE BEEN DEVISED, INCLUDING THIS SWEET, SYRUPY OFFERING.

honey	1/2 cup
sweet dark sherry, such as Pedro Ximénez	1/2 cup
ground cinnamon	1/4 teaspoon
dried figs	18 large
whole blanched almonds	18
dark chocolate	2/3 cup, cut into small pieces
heavy cream	for serving, optional

Combine the honey, sherry, cinnamon, and figs with 1 1/2 cups water in a large saucepan over high heat. Bring to a boil, then reduce the heat and simmer for 10 minutes. Remove the pan from the heat and set aside for 3 hours. Remove the figs with a slotted spoon, reserving the liquid.

Preheat the oven to 350°F. Return the pan of liquid to the stove and boil over high heat for 5 minutes or until syrupy, then set aside. Snip the stems from the figs with scissors, then cut a slit in the top of each fig with a small, sharp knife. Push an almond and a few shards of chocolate into each slit. Put the figs in a lightly buttered dish and bake for 15 minutes or until the chocolate has melted.

Serve three figs per person with a little of the sherry syrup poured over and a dollop of cream alongside, if using.

Each September, in the town of Lloret on the Spanish island of Majorca, there is a fiesta devoted to the fig. During this time you may try over sixty-three varieties of this luscious fruit and see the crowning of that year's Fig Princess. Walk anywhere in rural southern Spain during the summer and you will see trees heavy with the fruit. Enter any market and you can admire the bulging purple or green fruit laid lovingly side by side. When fresh, figs are eaten simply with cheese or slices of *jamón*. When dried, they are stuffed with everything from blue cheese to walnuts and honey, or packed into little cakes with bay leaves and fennel.

three ways with fruit

IN SUMMER, SPANISH MARKETS ARE FILLED WITH THE SCENT OF APRICOTS, PLUMS, PEACHES, PEARS, AND NECTARINES, AS WELL AS MELONS OF EVERY SHAPE AND COLOR. WITH SUCH A CORNUCOPIA OF FRUIT, IT COMES AS NO SURPRISE THAT FRUIT DESSERTS ABOUND. SIMPLICITY IS THE KEY, AS THESE RECIPES SHOW. THE FIRST OF THEM, PEARS COOKED IN RED WINE, IS A CATALAN CLASSIC; THE SECOND, *GAZPACHO DE FRUTAS*, IS FROM MAJORCA; AND THE THIRD IS A TRADITIONAL ASTURIAN RECIPE MADE DURING THE APPLE-PICKING CIDER SEASON.

pears cooked in red wine

Rub 4 peeled, firm, ripe pears with 1/3 cup lemon juice. Put 1 cup dry red wine, 2 cinnamon sticks, 1 cup sugar, 8 lemon slices, and 1 cup water in a saucepan over low heat and simmer gently until the sugar dissolves. Bring to a boil, then reduce the heat and simmer for about 15 minutes. Add the pears and simmer for another 20 minutes, carefully turning occasionally to ensure even browning. Remove the lemon slices and leave the pears to soak in the syrup overnight, if possible. Remove the pears and simmer the syrup over high heat for about 15 minutes or until it thickens slightly. Serve the pears whole, drizzled with the syrup. Serves 4.

gazpacho de frutas

Put 1 cup Pedro Ximénez sherry, 1 cup muscatel wine, and 2 cups of any other sweet wine you like (or use 4 cups total of the same wine) in a large bowl. Add 2 tablespoons sugar, 3/4 cup strawberries, and some slices of peeled peach, nectarines, melon, and plums—any summer fruit will do. Mix well, and leave in the refrigerator for 1 hour. Before serving, pour a bottle of *cava* (Catalan sparkling wine) over. Serves 8.

apple pudding

Peel, core, and slice 4 medium firm cooking apples. Put in a saucepan with 1/2 cup rum, mix together, and simmer until the apples are softened. In a separate saucepan, put 2 cups water with scant 1 cup sugar and heat, stirring constantly, until the sugar dissolves into a syrup. Add the syrup to the apples with another 1/2 cup rum, 4 egg yolks, 1/2 cup gelatin powder, and 1 teaspoon lemon juice. Purée the mixture in a blender or pass through a sieve. Dissolve another 1/3 cup sugar with 1/4 cup water in a small saucepan over low heat, stirring until the sugar dissolves (without boiling), then increase the heat and watch carefully until it caramelizes. Pour into a long heatproof mold (2 lb. 4 oz.) and swirl it around to coat the base and sides evenly. Pour over the apple mixture and cover with 6–8 ladyfinger cookies. Leave in the refrigerator for 8 hours or overnight and then turn out of the mold by putting a plate over it and flip it. Serve with fresh cream. Serves 6.

tocino de cielo

TRANSLATED AS "BACON FROM HEAVEN," THIS IS A POPULAR ANDALUSIAN RECIPE, OFTEN MADE BY THE NUNS IN THEIR CONVENTS. IT IS INDEED HEAVENLY, BUT ALSO SATISFYINGLY WICKED. IT IS TRADITIONALLY DECORATED WITH TINY MERINGUES, WHICH SIT ON TOP.

superfine sugar	1¼ cups
vanilla bean	1, sliced in half lengthwise
egg yolks	6
egg	1

Preheat the oven to 350ºF. Put 3 tablespoons water and ½ cup of the sugar in a small saucepan over low to medium heat. Stir with a metal spoon until all the sugar has dissolved. Bring to a boil and cook for another 10–15 minutes or until the toffee is a rich golden color. Remove from the heat, and taking care not to burn yourself, pour into an 8-inch square cake pan, tilting to cover the base.

Meanwhile, put 1 cup water in a saucepan with the vanilla bean and remaining sugar. Bring to a boil, then reduce the heat and simmer for 10 minutes or until the liquid has reduced to a slightly syrupy consistency. Allow to cool a little.

Using electric beaters, beat the egg yolks and whole egg until smooth. Slowly add a stream of the cooled sugar mixture while beating on high. Once combined, strain the liquid onto the toffee mixture in the cake pan.

Put the cake pan in a larger baking dish. Pour enough boiling water into the larger dish to come one-third of the way up the side of the cake pan. Bake for 30 minutes or until just set. Allow to cool completely before serving. When cold, dip the pan into a hot water bath for 30 seconds to loosen the caramel. Run a knife around the custard and unmold onto a serving plate. Drizzle any remaining caramel over the top and cut into small squares.

Tilt the cake pan to ensure the toffee covers the base evenly.

Add the sugar mixture to the eggs, beating constantly.

Strain the egg mixture into the pan, covering the cooled toffee.

leche frita .... serves 4 to 6

THIS TRADITIONAL RECIPE FOR "FRIED MILK" FOUND ALL OVER SPAIN (BUT ESPECIALLY IN THE NORTH) MARRIES CINNAMON AND VANILLA. IT CAN BE DIFFICULT TO MAKE THE FIRST TIME, BUT IT IS WELL WORTH THE EFFORT— ESPECIALLY IF YOU ARE COOKING FOR CHILDREN.

milk	2 cups
cinnamon stick	1
lemon zest	1 piece, about $1/2$ x 2 inches
vanilla bean	1, split and seeds scraped out
unsalted butter	10 tablespoons
all-purpose flour	2 cups
superfine sugar	$2/3$ cup
eggs	4, separated
dry breadcrumbs	$1 1/4$ cups
vegetable oil	for pan-frying
ground cinnamon	1 teaspoon, for dusting
superfine sugar	1 teaspoon, for dusting

Grease an 11 x 7-inch cake pan and line the base and long sides with baking paper. Put the milk, cinnamon stick, lemon zest, and scraped vanilla bean and seeds in a saucepan, and bring to a boil. Turn the heat off.

Melt the butter in a large, heavy-based saucepan. Stir in $1 1/2$ cups of the flour. The mixture will form a loose clump around your spoon. Stir over low heat for 30 seconds, then stir in the $2/3$ cup sugar. Gradually strain the milk into the pan, stirring constantly. Mix for about 10 minutes or until a smooth mass forms and it leaves the side of the pan. Remove from the heat and stir in the egg yolks one at a time, beating well after each addition (the mixture should now be quite glossy). Spread the custard mixture in the cake pan, smoothing the surface with your hand. Set aside for 1 hour to cool and set.

Lightly whisk the egg whites together with a fork. Lift the set custard from the pan and carefully cut into 2-inch squares. Dip in the remaining flour to coat all sides. Dip into the egg whites, then the breadcrumbs. Set aside.

Add the oil to a large frying pan to a depth of $1/2$ inch. Heat the oil, add a few custard squares at a time, and cook for 1 minute on each side or until browned. Drain on paper towels. Mix the sugar and cinnamon together and use to dust the squares while they are still hot. Serve hot or cold.

Add the flour to the butter, stirring with a wooden spoon.

Add the sugar and milk to the pan and stir until smooth.

Coat the custard squares in flour, then egg white and breadcrumbs.

three ways with citrus

THE BITTER ORANGE (TODAY KNOWN AS THE SEVILLE ORANGE) WAS THE FIRST ORANGE TO ARRIVE IN SPAIN, BROUGHT FROM CHINA BY THE MOORS IN THE TWELFTH CENTURY; SWEET ORANGES WOULD NOT ARRIVE FOR ANOTHER THREE HUNDRED YEARS. AN ORANGE GROVE WAS (AND STILL IS) PLANTED OUTSIDE THE ANCIENT MOSQUE, THE *MESQUITA*, IN CÓRDOBA, PROVIDING COLOR, FRAGRANCE, AND THIRST-SLAKING FRUIT TO WORSHIPERS. LIKE MUCH IN SPAIN, THE FOLLOWING RECIPES STRADDLE THE ANCIENT AND MODERN.

bizcocho

Preheat the oven to 315ºF. Using electric beaters, beat 6 eggs (at room temperature) and $1^2/_3$ cups superfine sugar for 15 minutes or until light and creamy. Beat in 2 teaspoons lemon zest. Using a large metal spoon or spatula, gently fold $1^1/_2$ cups sifted all-purpose flour into the egg mixture. Lightly grease and line a 9-inch springform cake pan. Pour in the batter and bake for 1 hour 10 minutes. Turn off the oven and leave the door open for 5 minutes, then remove the cake from the oven and allow to cool completely in the pan. Serves 8.

majorcan orange salad

Peel and cut 4 semiripe navel oranges into medium-thick slices and season with salt, white pepper (freshly ground if you have white peppercorns), and a little sugar. Finely chop the leaves of 2 mint sprigs and sprinkle them over the orange slices. Sprinkle $3/4$ cup good-quality pitted small black olives over the orange slices and add a generous dash of rich and fruity extra-virgin olive oil. Toss and refrigerate for 30 minutes. Serves 4.

oranges with coconut

Peel and cut 3 Valencia oranges into $1/2$-inch-thick slices and arrange on a platter. Sprinkle with 3 tablespoons sugar and 1 cup unsweetened coconut flakes. Stir and allow to sit for 30 minutes. Add a dollop of heavy cream to each slice and serve. Serves 4.

gypsy's arm cake .... serves 8 to 10

BRAZOS DE GITANO, AS THIS RICH DESSERT IS KNOWN IN SPAIN, IS A FAVORITE ON FEAST DAYS IN BARCELONA.
FOR THE FULL SPANISH EFFECT, TRY PEDRO XIMÉNEZ FOR THE TEASPOON OF RICH, SWEET SHERRY.

dark chocolate	1 1/3 cups, broken into pieces
strong black coffee	1/3 cup
eggs	7, brought to room temperature, then separated
superfine sugar	2/3 cup
confectioners' sugar	4 teaspoons
cocoa powder	3 tablespoons
rich, sweet sherry or rum	1 teaspoon
light cream	1 1/4 cups, whipped

Preheat the oven to 350°F. Grease a 13 x 9 inch jelly-roll pan and line with baking paper.

Melt the chocolate and coffee in a bowl over a small saucepan of simmering water, stirring occasionally, until almost melted. Take care the bowl does not touch the water. Remove from the heat and stir until smooth. Set aside to cool a little.

Beat the egg yolks and superfine sugar in a large bowl until light and creamy, then stir in the chocolate mixture. Whisk the egg whites in a separate bowl until soft peaks form. Using a large metal spoon or rubber spatula, gently fold the whites into the chocolate mixture. Pour the mixture into the lined pan and bake on the middle shelf of the oven for 15 minutes or until the cake springs back when lightly touched in the middle. Turn off the oven and open the door slightly.

After 10 minutes, remove the pan from the oven and turn out the cake onto a dish towel that has been dusted with the combined confectioners' sugar and cocoa powder. Allow to cool for 30 minutes.

Sprinkle the top of the sponge cake with the sherry and spread with the whipped cream. Roll the cake up, using the dish towel to help you, but removing it as you go. Wrap the cake in plastic wrap and refrigerate until ready to slice and serve.

Stir the chocolate mixture into the eggs and sugar.

Spread the cream over the cake, smoothing it with a knife.

Use a dish towel to help lift and roll the cake up.

torta de santiago

serves 8

SINCE MEDIEVAL TIMES, THE GALICIAN CITY OF SANTIAGO DE COMPOSTELA, IN SPAIN'S FAR NORTHWEST, HAS BEEN THE DESTINATION FOR THE MILLIONS OF PILGRIMS THAT HAVE WALKED THE PILGRIM'S WAY, STARTING FROM EITHER NAVARRA OR SOUTHERN FRANCE. AT THE END OF THEIR JOURNEY, THIS CAKE AWAITS THEM.

blanched whole almonds	3 cups, lightly roasted
unsalted butter	11 tablespoons, softened
superfine sugar	1³/4 cups
eggs	6
all-purpose flour	1¹/4 cups
lemon zest	2 teaspoons grated
lemon juice	3 tablespoons
confectioners' sugar	for dusting

Preheat the oven to 325°F. Lightly grease a 9-inch springform cake pan. Put the almonds in a food processor and grind until fine.

Using electric beaters, cream the butter and superfine sugar in a bowl until light and fluffy. Add the eggs one at a time, beating well after each addition. Using a metal spoon, fold in the flour, ground almonds, and the lemon zest. Stir until just combined and smooth.

Pour the batter into the cake pan and bake for 1 hour 20 minutes or until a skewer inserted into the center comes out clean. Cool for 5 minutes, then brush the top with lemon juice. Transfer to a wire rack and cool completely. Dust with confectioners' sugar in a cross pattern, using a stencil if desired.

In early spring, the plains outside Palma, the capital of Majorca, are a sea of white almond blossom. Majorca is one of the major Spanish producers of almonds, which, although introduced to Spain by the Moors, were not extensively planted on the island until the eighteenth century. Each year, in early August, the nuts are shaken to the ground, the tough green skins cut off, and the kernels left to dry in the sun before being sent for roasting or cracking. Today, mostly the soft-shelled varieties are farmed, but, if you look carefully, you can still find the more flavorful, if more difficult to open, hard-shelled almonds in specialty nut stores.

three ways with dessert sherry

THE SINGLE-VARIETY DESSERT SHERRIES MADE FROM EITHER PEDRO XIMÉNEZ OR MUSCAT GRAPES ARE ONLY NOW BEING DISCOVERED BY THE OUTSIDE WORLD. THEY ARE A REVELATION, CONTAINING THE DEPTH AND LAYERS OF SHERRY, BUT WITH AN ADDED RICH SWEETNESS. THIS RENEWED POPULARITY IS FORTUNATE, AS NOT LONG AGO, IT WAS SAID THAT THE PEDRO XIMÉNEZ GRAPE WAS NEARING EXTINCTION. TODAY, WINE LOVERS AND CHEFS ARE DISCOVERING THE VERSATILITY AND DELIGHTS OF THESE SHERRIES IN COOKING AND FOR DRINKING.

torrijas

Dip both sides of 4 thick slices of day-old bread in $3/4$ cup single-variety dessert sherry, then drizzle any leftover liquid over them. Allow the bread to sit for a few minutes to absorb the sherry. Heat $1/4$ cup olive oil in a frying pan over medium heat. Beat 2 eggs with a dash of milk, then dip the bread slices into the egg. Fry the bread on each side for 3–4 minutes or until golden brown. Drain on paper towels, then dust with 1 teaspoon ground cinnamon mixed with 2 tablespoons superfine sugar or, if you prefer, drizzle with honey. Serves 4.

drunken cakes

Cut 1 bizcocho (page 175), baked in a square or rectangular pan, into squares. Put $1/2$ cup superfine sugar and $1/2$ cup water in a small saucepan over low heat and stir with a metal spoon until the sugar has dissolved. Bring to a boil for 4 minutes. Add $1/2$ cup single-variety dessert sherry and boil for 3 minutes or until syrupy. Drizzle the syrup evenly over the cake squares. Dust the tops with ground cinnamon and serve with whipped cream. Serves 8–10.

pedro ximénez with chocolate

Rich, dark, and exquisite, Pedro Ximénez sherry (pronounced "shimeneth") is largely unknown in the non-Spanish world. Mysterious and exotic, it has a secret of its own: it loves chocolate. Pour it over chocolate ice cream or a chocolate dessert, add it to a recipe for chocolate cake, soak lightly stewed plums in it and eat them with something chocolate, and, in winter, add it to hot chocolate. Now you know.

polvorones .... makes 20

THIS DISH TAKES ITS NAME FROM THE WORD *POLVO*, MEANING "POWDER"—*POLVORONES* ARE VERY FRAGILE AND BURST DELIGHTFULLY IN THE MOUTH AS YOU EAT THEM. THEY ARE ANOTHER SPANISH SWEET THAT COMES INTO ITS OWN AT CHRISTMAS AND EASTER.

all-purpose flour	2 cups, sifted
ground aniseed	1/2 teaspoon
confectioners' sugar	1 cup, sifted
butter	1 cup plus 2 tablespoons, softened
egg yolk	1
lemon juice	1 teaspoon
dry sherry	2 teaspoons

In a large bowl combine the flour, aniseed, 4 teaspoons of the confectioners' sugar, and a pinch of salt.

Beat the butter with electric beaters until pale and creamy, then beat in the egg yolk, lemon juice, and sherry until well combined. Beat in half the flour mixture with the electric beaters, then stir in the remaining flour with a wooden spoon. Gather the dough into a ball with your hands, cover with plastic wrap, and refrigerate for 1 hour. Preheat the oven to 300°F.

Roll out the dough on a floured surface to 1/2 inch thick. Using a 2-inch cutter, cut into cookies. Transfer to an ungreased cookie sheet and bake for 20 minutes or until the cookies are light brown and firm. Allow to cool slightly, then roll the cookies in the remaining confectioners' sugar. Reserve any remaining confectioners' sugar. Cool completely, then roll in the confectioners' sugar again. Store the cookies, covered with any remaining confectioners' sugar, for up to 2 weeks in an airtight container.

Stir in the last of the flour mixture to make a dough.

Use a dough cutter to cut out rounds of pastry.

Bake the cookies, then roll them in sugar, coating all over.

aniseed cookies..makes 16

THESE SIMPLE COOKIES ARE MADE MORE INTRIGUING WITH THE ADDITION OF ANISEED, WHICH GIVES THEM A SWEET LICORICE EDGE. THEY ARE GOOD AT ANY TIME OF THE DAY AND WOULD MAKE A DELICIOUS ACCOMPANIMENT TO A *CARAJILLO*, A SHORT, BLACK COFFEE LACED WITH ANISE.

all-purpose flour	3 cups
olive oil	1/2 cup
beer	1/2 cup
anisette liqueur	1/4 cup
superfine sugar	1/2 cup
sesame seeds	1/4 cup
aniseeds	3 tablespoons

Preheat the oven to 400°F. Lightly grease a cookie sheet and line with baking paper.

Sift the flour and 1 teaspoon salt into a large bowl and make a well. Add the oil, beer, and anisette liqueur and mix with a large metal spoon until the dough comes together. Transfer to a lightly floured surface and knead for about 3–4 minutes or until smooth. Divide the dough in half, then divide each half into 8 portions.

In a small bowl, combine the sugar, sesame seeds, and aniseeds.

Make a small pile of the seed mixture on a work surface and roll out each portion of dough over the mixture to a 6-inch round, embedding the seeds underneath. Put the rounds on the cookie sheet, with the seeds on top, and cook for 5–6 minutes or until the bases are crisp. Put the cookies under a broiler for about 40 seconds or until the sugar caramelizes and the surface is golden. Transfer to a wire rack to cool.

Although aniseed is an important ingredient in some desserts, it is more often seen as a liqueur in Spain, as anise. When you see old men sitting around in cafés in the villages, they will, more than likely, have a small glass of anise in front of them. Although each region has its specialty—in Majorca, for example, they add aromatic herbs like rosemary and fennel to make a drink called *hierbas*—there are also the national brands. Perhaps the most famous of these are Chinchón (named after the town near Madrid) and Anis del Mono.

magdalenas

Every afternoon, Spanish schoolchildren run home to their mothers for the *merienda* (afternoon snack), which will often feature these little cakes. Similarly, when they visit their *abuelas* (grandmothers), the first thing they will be given is a handful of magdalenas. This delicious little cake, here made using olive oil and a little lemon zest, is as much a part of the childhood memories of most Spaniards as the madeleine (a close relation) was for Marcel Proust whose book *Remembrance of Things Past* was famously provoked by the aroma of the little cake dipped in tea.

Magdalenas are another example, like the tortilla, of the "direct and simple" school of Spanish culinary art. They are also, again like the tortilla, difficult to perfect. This recipe will help you in your attempts.

Preheat the oven to 375°F. Mix 1¾ cups all-purpose flour, a heaping ⅓ cup superfine sugar, and the grated zest of 1 lemon together in a bowl. Add 3 tablespoons milk, ¾ cup plus 1 tablespoon olive oil, and 6 egg yolks. Mix until smooth. In a separate bowl, whisk 6 egg whites until stiff, then add half to the olive-oil mixture and beat in. Add the remaining beaten egg whites and mix thoroughly until smooth. Spoon the mixture into a well-greased 12-cup muffin or mini-loaf pan and bake them for 20–25 minutes. Serve warm, straight from the oven. They will collapse slightly as they cool. Makes 12.

almond *turrón* ice cream

THIS IS A COOL SUMMER VERSION OF *TURRÓN*, WHICH, IF THE MOORS DIDN'T THINK OF IT, THEY CERTAINLY SHOULD HAVE. USE PEDRO XIMÉNEZ OR MUSCATEL SHERRY IN THE RECIPE IF YOU CAN.

superfine sugar	½ cup, plus ⅓ cup, extra
blanched almonds	⅓ cup, roasted
egg yolks	6
sweet sherry	⅓ cup plus 1 tablespoon
light cream	1¾ cups

To make the almond praline, combine the ½ cup sugar and ¼ cup water in a saucepan. Stir over low heat with a metal spoon until the sugar has dissolved. Increase the heat, bring to a boil and cook for 6 minutes or until the mixture is dark golden brown (but not burned). Sprinkle the almonds onto a greased cookie sheet, then pour on the toffee and set aside to harden.

Mix the egg yolks and ⅓ cup sugar in a bowl with an electric beater until pale and creamy. Whisk in the sherry. Transfer the custard to a heatproof bowl over a saucepan of simmering water, making sure the bowl does not touch the water. Whisk constantly for about 12 minutes or until the custard is thick and foamy. Remove from the heat at this point, cover and leave to cool.

Whip the cream until firm, but not stiff. When the custard is cool, gently fold in the cream using a large metal spoon or spatula until combined. Pour the mixture into a shallow metal container such as a cake pan with a 4-cup capacity. Chill until frozen around the edges. Tip into a bowl and beat with an electric mixer until smooth. Tip the custard back into the container and refreeze. Repeat this process three times, or until the ice cream is soft.

Crush the praline and fold it through the ice cream after the final mixing. For the final freezing, put the ice cream in an airtight container and cover with a piece of waxed paper and a lid. Freeze for at least 3 hours, or until set.

To make the praline, pour the hot toffee over the almonds.

Set the custard over simmering water and whisk until thick.

Beat the chilled ice cream until smooth, then refreeze it.

index

Thunder Bay Press
An imprint of the Advantage Publishers Group
5880 Oberlin Drive, San Diego, CA 92121-4794
www.thunderbaybooks.com

Copyright © Murdoch Books Pty Limited, 2005

Copyright under International, Pan American, and Universal Copyright Conventions. All rights reserved. No part of this book may be reproduced or transmitted in any form or by any means, electronic or mechanical, including photocopying, recording, or by any information storage-and-retrieval system, without written permission from the copyright holder. Brief passages (not to exceed 1,000 words) may be quoted for reviews.

All notations of errors or omissions should be addressed to Thunder Bay Press, Editorial Department, at the above address. All other correspondence (author inquiries, permissions) concerning the content of this book should be addressed to Murdoch Books Pty Limited, Pier 8/9 23 Hickson Road, Millers Point NSW 2000 Australia.

ISBN 1-59223-402-X
Library of Congress Cataloging-in-Publication Data available upon request.

Printed in China.
1 2 3 4 5   09 08 07 06 05

IMPORTANT: Those who might be at risk from the effects of salmonella poisoning (the elderly, pregnant women, young children, and those suffering from immune deficiency diseases) should consult their doctor with any concerns about eating raw eggs.

CONVERSION GUIDE: You may find cooking times vary depending on the oven you are using. For convection ovens, as a general rule, set the oven temperature to 70°F lower than indicated in the recipe.